GO
TELL IT!

How a Surrendered Life Can Transform Lives
and the World One Story at a Time

DEBBY EFURD

Clovercroft Publishing

Go Tell It! How a Surrendered Life Can Transform Lives
and the World One Story at a Time

© 2015 by Debby Efurd

Scripture taken from the NEW AMERICAN STANDARD BIBLE®, Copyright ©
1960,1962,1963,1968,1971,1972,1973,1975,1977,1995 by The Lockman
Foundation. Used by permission.

Published by Clovercroft Publishing, Franklin, Tennessee

Published in association with Larry Carpenter of Christian Book Services, LLC
www.christianbookservices.com

Cover Design and Interior Layout Design by Suzanne Lawing

Edited by Tammy Kling

Printed in the United States of America

978-1-942557-01-2

WHAT PEOPLE ARE SAYING ABOUT *GO TELL IT!*

"Debby Efurd shares her surrendered life with transparency and humility in a way that will touch your heart as she encourages you to share your own journey of faith. *Go Tell It!* is a marvelous example of the power a transformed life can make on individuals and our culture. This book is a must-read for everyone."

—Dr. Robert Jeffress, senior pastor,
First Baptist Church, Dallas, Texas

"What a pleasure to recommend Debby Efurd's work of the heart, *Go Tell It!* Debby writes as if one were sitting down having a conversation over coffee with a trusted friend, making her book one that's easy to read, heartwarming, and intimate. That's not an easy feat when covering the often taboo subject of abortion: a subject not discussed in polite company or in your church and Bible study circles! But honorably and with honesty, Debby shines light into the darkness of many women's darkest secret and shows the miraculous transformation that comes when we allow the Lord to heal our greatest hurts and then choose to declare His greatness and graciousness in doing so.

"May we all choose to be so vulnerable and bold in sharing our own stories of restoration and healing in Jesus' name! Thank you, Debby, for leading the way with this beautiful tribute to life and the One who gives it."

—Carolyn Cline-Hollis, president and CEO,
Involved for Life, Inc. (Downtown Pregnancy
Center, Uptown Women's Center, and
Sonograms On Site), Dallas, Texas

"There's nothing like living in the most marvelous of places of God's grace, mercy, and love while escaping our self-imposed prison of regret and shame. Debby Efurd's transparent story shines with the magnificent light of God, growing ever brighter with every personal error of judgment she reveals. *Go Tell It!* is a wonderful book which details how a person's simple story can affect another individual and the eventual impact that can have on the world. I encourage everyone to read this compelling story. Good job, Debby!"

—Carol Everett, founder and president, The Heidi Group, Round Rock, Texas

"*Go Tell It!* is a powerful and honest account of accepting forgiveness resulting in the miraculous, healing power of God. Debby Efurd uniquely shares how her story began a good work and how that work blossomed to impact the lives of others. She gives true-life testimonials that provide a deeper understanding of grief and its consequences. Biblical reflection and useful steps help us better understand God's love and the power of sharing our stories. Go Tell It! is a marvelous reminder that God wants to redeem pain in our lives and use it for His glory. I highly recommend this book."

—Dr. Cynthia Mickens Ross, speaker, author, pastor: Pathway to Purpose, Pathway to Life Center of Hope

"With breathtaking honesty, Debby Efurd peels back the layers of her roller-coaster life and leaves surprising lessons in the reader's heart. How many people do you know who have negotiated abortion, loss of their home, substance abuse, single motherhood, divorce, marital mental aberrations, breast cancer, and the creativity of entrepreneurial compassion and who yet wants to share the tale?

"After turning over all the rocks in her pilgrimage, she was led by her solid Christian faith to accept the forgiveness of God and to seal it by proffering that same forgiveness to everyone who abandoned her in her need. The "Rickey story" is an indelible example. The spiritual testimonies alone are, by themselves, worth the price of the book!

"If you are a counselor, pastor, teacher, church staff member, or just a friend who cares for those caught up in the quagmires of life, you need what *Go Tell It!* has in your arsenal of empathy and your library of love."

 —Dr. Dan L. Griffin, pastor, First Baptist
  Church, Lancaster, Texas

"Debby Efurd should be applauded for taking an emotionally painful experience that many hide away and bringing it out in the open so women know they are not alone. Her candid retelling of her own story, post abortion, as well as the stories of others who have found healing will help any woman who still struggles. Through Efurd's book, we once again see that the only way to overcome our greatest trials is through the strength and love of Jesus Christ."

 —Lisa Burkhardt Worley, co-author of
  the award-winning book *If I Only Had . . .*
  Wrapping Yourself in God's Truth During
  Storms of Insecurity and *the Pearls of*
  Promise devotional

"The first time I met Debby Efurd was via the "big" screen at the church we both attend. I was awestruck by her willingness to divulge her secret of abortion. That takes courage and a confirmation of a surrendered life. Debby is a modern-day "woman at the well"! After she confessed and received forgiveness for this "secret" sin, she, like the woman at the well, could not remain silent about how God brought hope, health, and healing into her life! Go Tell It! is a MUST-read for everyone. Its author shares the voices of many who have received parole from their guilty verdicts from within the prison cells in which their hearts have been locked up because of guilt and shame! Debby freely shares the keys to unlocking the door to your heart to find peace that only JESUS can give after the storms in your life."

—MARILYN MANSFIELD, FOUNDER AND PRESIDENT, M3 COMMUNICATIONS, DALLAS, TEXAS

"What a powerful testimony of God's love and forgiveness. In *Go Tell It!*, Debby Efurd honestly recounts sinful choices in her life that resulted in devastating consequences as she details her journey to accept God's forgiveness and peace. She shares how God is using her surrendered life for His glory and purpose and demonstrates that all of us have the power to impact others and the world by simply sharing our personal stories of faith and redemption."

—JOHN AND LORRAINE MUTSCH, CO-FOUNDERS, RENATI PARTNERS, DALLAS, TEXAS

ACKNOWLEDGMENTS

Where do I start in expressing my gratitude?

To my God, who gave me transformation and hope for living, thank You for loving me before I could love myself.

To Cary, my husband, my soul mate, my best friend—thank you for believing in me always and being my sounding board.

To my children and grandchildren—you make me want to be the best I can be, as you inspire me to leave a strong legacy for you. Thank you for putting up with me in my ups and downs and always, always encouraging me to keep on keeping on.

To the countless friends who pray for and with me—your prayers have carried me through the roller coasters of life. My heart overflows when I think of my many prayer warriors.

To the multitude of ministry leaders whose advice and guidance have been so invaluable, thank you for your God-given wisdom and encouragement.

To the many who inspired and believed in me from the First Baptist Church of Dallas music ministry. It was the example of many of you in the choir and orchestra who inspired me to step out in faith and share my story publicly.

To the board members and volunteers of the collective ministries of **Initiative 180** and **Peace After the Storm**—your stories are a beautiful reminder to me of the power of a personal testimony.

DEDICATION

This book is dedicated to those who have found their voice by publicly sharing their personal testimony, and in so doing, boldly point to Jesus Christ, who gives victory and the power to overcome. Keep sharing those stories! You inspire unknown multitudes of family, friends, coworkers, and strangers to start their own journey and find their lost voices.

CONTENTS

FOREWORD

One beautiful day in spring, I sat in this well-decorated, colorful kitchen, not really knowing why I was there but understanding that I was invited by a precious new friend whom I had grown to highly respect. She told me I needed to meet the person who was the speaker for that particular get-together. I almost chickened out of going because I considered myself too busy to sit at a tea-like gathering on a Saturday with people I hardly knew . . . or did not know at all. But I didn't want to disappoint my new friend. So I showed up. The atmosphere was cheerful and relaxing, which helped me settle down and prepare to listen to this lady who was unknown to me. Immediately, as Debby began to speak, I knew I should sit up, pay attention, listen, glean, and learn about what she was saying—not only because her message shocked me but also because I needed to take heed about the virtues of her experiences. Amazed, surprised, stunned, saddened, startled, condemned, enlightened, encouraged, and empowered describes my reactions to her moving message. I was spellbound!

Now that you have the blessing of Debby's full story, I invite you to not only read this honest and compelling trail of circumstances, intrigue, and power but also to embrace the life lessons from Debby's experiences that are backed by the inspired word of God. As the song says, "Go Tell It on the Mountain!" Yes, tell her story over the hills, valleys, nations, and everywhere. This news is vital for generations now and those to come. This legacy of a roller-coaster life, if taken to heart, can guide you through the crooks and turns, valleys and hills, and hopes and dreams of your life to the reality of a solid road of peace, honesty, wholeness, virtue, and inward freedom.

What Debby offered to me the day I met her motivated me

to look deep within my being and to honestly analyze my life experiences to see how they can shape my life every day . . . and how I can grow from them. Over the years of my experiences, through Debby's story you can begin to be honest about your circumstances, your vulnerabilities, and the truths you can gain from the words from Debby's life. When I speak throughout the United States and other parts of the world, I often remember the lessons learned from Debby's lips and know I can take these lessons with me in this life-changing book. Debby has empowered me to "Go Tell It!"

—Dr. Thelma ("Mama T") Wells, DD, CEO, That A Girl & Friends Speakers Agency and A Woman of God Ministries; author, speaker, mentor, professor

INTRODUCTION

My fondest memories as a child were times spent with my grandmother. With her, I felt safe. She was a refuge the many times my mother shuttled my brother and me to our grandmother's house after my parents had an "argument."

I can still smell the aroma from her kitchen. She was the best cook in the world. Her pot roast with brown gravy, her fresh-made rolls and butter, her rice pudding, and her specialty— peach cobbler!

I remember the house filled with fresh-cut flowers. Her starched sheets created a natural "slip and slide" when I jumped on the bed. That was the best sleep in the world: on starched sheets next to a window where the gentle summer wind blew across the bed.

But nothing compared to her stories. Curling up in her lap, pressing against her soft, generous flesh . . . her arms were so fun to wiggle! She read me countless fairy tales and fables and told me stories from her youth. She swept me off to a make-believe world, one where everyone lived happily ever after.

It's a funny thing about stories. Just about every story I have heard are alike in that they have the same elements of **Control** . . . **Choice** . . . and **Consequence**. Looking back in my own life, that's what happened to me. I took **Control** . . . I made a **Choice** . . . and I bore the **Consequences**. Some of those consequences resulted in years of guilt, shame, and regret that robbed me of real joy in life, holding onto a secret so tight I thought I would carry it to my grave.

But that wasn't God's plan. And so my journey began . . .

PART I

LEARN IT!

Going through a waiting period doesn't mean there is nothing happening, because when you are waiting on the Lord, He is always moving in your life.
—STORMIE OMARTIAN

January 2013

As long as I can remember, I wanted to be on the radio. Arriving early at the radio station, I was a bundle of nerves as I mentally prepared for the recording session.

I had so many questions. Would I stumble over my words? Would I even be coherent? What would the radio host ask me?

But the biggest question of all was . . . how had I gotten here?

—Debby

CHAPTER 1
The Formative Years

Your hands made me and fashioned me; give me
understanding, that I may learn Your commandments.
—PSALM 119:73, NEW AMERICAN STANDARD BIBLE

Deborah Jan Ferrell was born October 24, 1951, in Dallas, Texas, at Methodist Hospital. That's me. My dad (Linden Aubrey, or "LA") was forty-five when I was born and my mom (Janis) was thirty-nine. My parents were older than the parents of all of my friends—mainly because they had both been previously married. I had a half-sister (Betty) and a half-brother (Jack) from my dad and mom, respectively. We were a blended family before that term became common. Actually, we were more like a family bush than a family tree. I knew both my parents had multiple marriages, but it wasn't until I was sixteen when I learned my dad had been married another time. Even my grandmother had had a divorce, at a time when divorce was unheard of.

I grew up during what many called the "Cold War, counterculture, and civil rights" era. In the decades following World War II, the US became a global influence in economics, politics, the military, culture, and technology. It was an era that saw the space race, the Vietnam War, the Cuban missile crisis, the assassination of President John F. Kennedy, the assassination of Dr. Martin Luther King, and the assassination of Attorney General Robert F. Kennedy.

Yes, I grew up in an era of "flower children, hippies, and free love." From 1951 on, there were many changes in the nation and the world as well as in our culture. What did this cultural shift mean to me? For one, it created the perfect environment for me to be rebellious. That word "rebellious" fit me to a "T."

My first "home" was actually my grandmother's house. She lived exactly one mile from our home in North Oak Cliff, a Dallas suburb. My mother took me straight to my grandmother's house from the hospital because my dad was taking care of his mother (Nettie). I never had the opportunity to meet Nettie . . . she died three weeks after I was born. I wish I had met her; the stories I was told about her made her sound like she was a very strong woman who took care of her large brood single-handedly. My favorite "Nettie" saying that my dad told me over and over again was "I am what I am, but I ain't no am-mer." It would be years before I fully understood and appreciated what that meant.

As I grew up, I don't remember many happy times at home, but I do remember loving my grandparents' house. I was there a lot. My grandmother Bom-Bom, as my brother and I called her, and Ninny, our grandfather, doted on us. Yes, the sun rose and set on their daughter, my mother, and my brother and me.

I was raised in Oak Cliff, "across the Trinity River." I lived blocks from the Texas Theater, which would later become famous in 1963 when Lee Harvey Oswald was arrested. I remember trolley cars on Jefferson Boulevard, spending Sundays at Polar Bear Ice Cream, and trips for snow cones at Aunt Stelle's.

My parents loved me, without a doubt. I was the baby of the

family. They saw to it I went to church every week, took every kind of lesson imaginable, practiced the piano daily, and earned my Girl Scout badges. We would take Sunday "drives" all the way to a little town south of Dallas called Duncanville.

I grew up attending Cliff Temple Baptist Church. My mother had me enrolled in the Cradle Roll (babies), Cherub Choir, Girl's Auxiliary, Training Union, and Vacation Bible School. In between being at church, I had dance lessons (tap, ballet, jazz), piano lessons, roller skating, two ice skating lessons, and four bowling lessons. Obviously, I didn't catch on to ice skating and bowling very well.

I remember a lot of the time, our family was loving. But the times when there were fights (and there were many), everything seemed to turn upside down. In my home there were undercurrents of dysfunction and conflict. Everyone walked on eggshells. Anger was internalized, but there were always the eventual eruptions. I didn't like the conflict, but I didn't know families could be different than mine. I thought all families fought, left, returned, tried to make up, then fought some more. I thought everyone kept secrets, never expressed feelings, avoided conflict, internalized anger, and blew up like a volcano.

My grandparents were a rock for me. It was there we would flee when my parents had a fight. It was there I spent holidays and most summers. We would go to East Texas to see my Aunt Dodie, spend time in the country, and hear the best stories ever! My grandfather would take me to fishing rodeos. I even won first place for catching the most sun perch in thirty minutes. To win a prize for fishing was amazing, seeing how I refused to bait the hook or touch the fish. Just like my grandmother Nettie, my grandmother Bom had favorite sayings. My favorite was "You can't make a silk purse out of a sow's ear." I could never quite figure out how a pig's ear could become a purse.

I was raised to be a "model" child and was expected to be

prim, proper, and perfect in all things. Naturally, I fell short . . . who could possibly be perfect? So when mistakes were made, and they happened often, someone had to be the scapegoat, and it usually fell on some poor, unsuspecting soul (like one of my friends). "Looking good" and "putting a good face on" was of primary importance to my mom. As I thought about it, she was probably trying to live her life through me.

My first experience of real fear came on April 2, 1957. It was a normal spring day. Mom was cooking dinner and I was watching American Bandstand. Then the TV and lights went off. It was dark in the house without electricity, but not as dark as it was outside. Mom ran through the living room, scooped me up, and we went out on the front porch. The sky was pea green; the trees, unnaturally still, without a single leaf moving. It was like all the air had been sucked out of the sky. My mother ran to a neighbor's house, found my brother, and dragged him home. I could see the fear in her eyes. I wanted to cry, but I was too scared. We heard the tornado long before we saw it. There it was . . . a huge funnel with all kinds of stuff whirling around the top, filled with breaking glass and popping noises. What lasted a few minutes seemed like an eternity. As soon as the tornado passed, we hopped in the car and drove to my dad's service station, or what was left of it. Police and ambulances were everywhere. All of Dad's employees narrowly escaped the tornado by running for cover, all except Big Willy. He was too loyal to my dad to leave for safety's sake. Daddy, thankfully, had left earlier to pick up parts for the station. If he had been at the service station, I often wondered if he would have run for cover or stayed with Big Willy. The fear I felt was etched permanently in my memory. Now every time I hear a tornado siren or we are under an alert, my heart starts racing. That's what real fear can do.

Growing up, I was always afraid I would say or do the wrong

thing and upset my parents, causing an outburst. When my parents had a fight, my mother was the one who left, gathering my brother and me and driving to my grandparents' house. In a few days (or a few weeks), my parents would make up, and we'd go back home and never talk about what happened. Within a month or two, there would be another argument and another trip to grandmother's.

My family was small in number. When I was a teenager, I discovered that both my mom and dad had cut themselves off from other family members. As an adult, I would meet members of the family I never knew and remember wishing I had had the chance to know them when I was younger. No cousins, one uncle, one aunt. Fights in the extended family had been going on for years. Those relationships were never restored.

When I was in the fourth grade, my parents divorced. They remarried after a year, remained married for thirteen years, and then divorced again. You could definitely call their relationship a roller coaster (about the size of the "Goliath" at Six Flags Magic Mountain). I remember my dad was angry a lot. My mother told me he drank, but I never witnessed his drinking. All I saw were the results of their relationship—arguing, running away, attempts at short-lived reconciliation, and the insecurity I felt.

At age seventeen, I tried to run away from home. One day, when my parents were working and I was supposed to be at school, I took my dad's car and headed to Kentucky, where my brother lived. I only made it as far as Texarkana, though, before I ran out of money and headed back home. I thought I had gotten away with my little "escapade," but my dad got home early that day, leaned against the car, felt the hot engine, and then checked the mileage. I was caught!

I grew up feeling insecure and looked for comfort wherever I could find it. I found that comfort in food. It made me feel good about myself and was my "go to" during conflicts in our home. But the more I ate, the more weight I gained, so my weight battle only added fuel to the fire to an already low sense of self-esteem. I wanted to have friends and be accepted so desperately. But in my family, we never expressed our feelings—we just "stuffed" them. So, holding onto secrets and never "talking" through conflict, I suppose it was natural for me to turn to food for comfort. I succeeded at eating . . . very well. As a teenager, my Mom found a doctor who prescribed "miracle diet pills" for weight loss. They worked, I lost the weight, and boys started noticing me.

Since I was a little girl I was told "how pretty I was," which was odd, because when I looked in the mirror, I never saw pretty . . . I saw fat and ugly. That translated to . . . "Who could ever love me?" Self-esteem . . . it's so important for people to feel good about themselves . . . to be emotionally healthy. Those same feelings of low self-worth would contribute to choices later in life that I would regret for a very long time.

After high school graduation, I attended Dallas Fashion Merchandising College, thinking I would earn my keep as a high-powered fashion buyer. I learned quickly that definitely wasn't my path and started attending Mountain View Junior College for business courses. My plan was to get a great job, earn lots of money, and move out on my own.

Growing up, I did what every child does—repeat patterns set for them. I modeled what I saw: I kept secrets, was manipulative, put on a good "face," kept feelings to myself, avoided conflict, and if there was conflict, I ran away and hid.

* * *

A child grows up thinking parents are perfect, but truth be told, parents are never perfect—they are human. Anyone who walks the face of this earth has imperfections patterned from those they surround themselves with. This is a lesson to all parents to set

26

good examples for your family. If you exhibit anger, anger will be the result.

However perfect or imperfect my parents may have been, they managed to plant little mustard seeds of faith, and God saw to it that they grew. Now that I am older, I am thankful to have been blessed with the parents He made just for me.

CHAPTER 2
The Rebellious Years

So I spoke to you, but you would not listen.
Instead you rebelled against the command of the LORD,
and acted presumptuously and went up into the hill country.
—DEUTERONOMY 1:43

PREGNANCY

I was twenty-one when I finally moved away from home. My dad didn't want me to leave; he even offered to build my own "wing and entrance" if I would stay home. But I had a job and money to spend, and I desperately wanted my own space so I could be in control. This was my time!

I moved, carrying my baggage of low self-worth with me. I began going out with friends, looking for acceptance in all the wrong places. I was the classic rebellious kid. Anything can become a habit—even habits that are against your very nature, if you practice them long enough—and that's what happened to me. I was always looking for someone to love me.

I met Rickey on a blind date. He showed me attention . . . he told me he loved me . . . wanted to spend the rest of his life with me . . . said I was his perfect match. I fell head over heels. Looking for my fairy-tale romance, here at last was my Prince

Charming. One thing led to another, and then one day I discovered I was pregnant. Oh no!

When I told Rickey I was pregnant, he told me he was married. He and his wife were separated, and he hadn't gotten around to getting a divorce. What? This didn't happen in any of the fairy tales I had read. What was I going to do? I couldn't have a baby! I couldn't tell my parents or anyone else for that matter; I was too embarrassed about what people would think of me. I was alone, scared, and naive. How could I have been so stupid? Is this what I get for trying to be in control? I confided in a coworker that I was pregnant and asked her what I should do. She wasn't shocked; in fact, she told me, quite nonchalantly, just to have an abortion. Abortion was now legal in the US and that would take care of my "problem." She said that she had had an abortion, and it was no big deal.

It was a Saturday morning in June 1973. I drove alone to the abortion clinic. Despite a picture-perfect day outside, for me it was dark and oppressive. When I arrived at the clinic, no one spoke to me; no one held my hand. I sat alone, waiting to be called for my appointment. I remember the sterile smell, the sounds, and the whir of the vacuum. Then the doctor told me, "Good news, you don't have a baby anymore." I wanted to throw up. I couldn't breathe as hot tears streamed down my cheeks.

After the procedure, I was escorted out the rear entry to the alley. Alone in my car, I sat and cried for what seemed an eternity. I kept telling myself, "Get a grip. No one has to know. You can go on with your life. You can forget about this." But that was the farthest thing from the truth.

There were two deaths that day in June 1973—my baby's and mine. Little by little, bottling up all emotion, I stopped crying and laughing for years. I shut myself off from friends and family; I didn't look people in the eye for fear they would see me for who I was and what I had done, a selfish person more concerned about myself than an innocent baby. I became a robot. My self-esteem hit rock bottom. I soon turned to every external comfort I could find to soothe my inner pain, building up walls around me as defenses to hide my shame and guilt.

Some post-abortive symptoms started immediately, while others lay dormant for years. I eventually sought help for the depression, the eating disorder, and the other problems that were affecting my life, but I never really followed up on the counseling for various reasons. I never connected the dots of all of my symptoms until years later, choosing to keep my secret protected and telling no one, not even my doctor. I put my physical and emotional health at risk because I didn't recognize the root problem—my abortion.

For a few weeks after the abortion, I felt relief, but that soon turned into regret. Dragging my "baggage" with me, I began numbing my pain through external comforts. I drank too much, partied too much, and took drugs to wake up and go to sleep. I lashed out at family, friends, and coworkers in anger, was depressed, and at times, even considered suicide. Decades later, I had flashbacks and nightmares about the abortion. But worst of all, this affected my relationship with the ones I loved over much of my adult life.

Yes, I had many symptoms of an underlying problem, which continued to rear its ugly head in intervals. Mostly I was angry and bitter, abusing anyone and everyone who crossed my path. But I continued to hold onto my secret of abortion because I didn't want to be judged. I had to be "perfect" to the world.

* * *

It would be thirty-five years before I made the connection . . . learning that most of the problems I faced stemmed from my choice of abortion. How I wish someone had told me the facts surrounding the lifelong effects from that one decision. How many millions had suffered like me?

MARRIAGE

In my rebellious spirit—and in wanting to prove to my parents, family, friends, and the rest of the world that I really did know what was best for me—Rickey and I married after his divorce became final. Yes, he was seven years older than me; yes, he had been married four times before; yes, he had children from previous marriages; yes, he didn't handle conflict well. I threw the warning signs out the window because I wanted to be loved first and foremost, so I clung to the first guy who looked my way. "After all," I told myself, "love does heal all wounds."

Rickey and I got married in jeans and tie-dyed shirts by a justice of the peace, not exactly my dream wedding. When my dad found out we had eloped, he disowned me, wrote me out of his will, and refused to talk to me or allow me to see my mother and grandmother. I was estranged from my parents and grandmother for several years.

During this time, Rickey started drinking heavily, which always meant his violent side would come out. I was alone in an abusive relationship with no one to turn to. Verbal and physical abuse were frightening, and that alone humbled me enough to seek help and reconcile with my parents. Yes, I ignored many warning signs because I was determined to get married. I didn't want to be an "old maid" and thought "love could change all." To be honest, I thought I could change Rickey.

Rickey was not a bad person. There were many good periods in our marriage, but when adversity struck—loss of a job, conflict with family—old habits would rear their ugly head, turning bad situations to worse.

* * *

Marriage is one of the biggest decisions anyone makes in life.
When a person marries, they marry that person's family, too.
Emotional maturity is so important in making wise decisions.
Over time, people do change, and fortunately, Rickey and I made
much-needed amends to one another later in our lives.

JACK

My brother Jack (actually my half-brother), was nine years older than me. I idolized him. He was a look-alike for Ricky Nelson and Elvis Presley. He was everything I wanted to be: good looking, successful, funny, and adored by everyone. He even took me to my senior prom (after my boyfriend and I broke up). No one knew he was my brother, but everyone thought I had a really hot date.

In the early hours of Saturday, November 15, 1975, I got a phone call. My sister-in-law's parents told me that Jack had been killed in an accident the night before while on a hunting trip. The Jeep he was travelling in had overturned, and Jack was thrown out the back seat, killing him instantly. I later learned that the driver, his boss, had been drinking.

I was devastated. Jack and I had spoken just a few days earlier and were looking forward to Thanksgiving. He had a wife . . . a young daughter . . . a wonderful life . . . everyone loved him. How could this happen to someone so good? God, where were you? Why didn't you protect him?

One of the hardest things I've ever had to do in my life was to tell my mother and grandmother that the apple of their eye, their beloved son and grandson, had been killed. Telling them, seeing their faces, was torture. What I didn't know then was how this tragedy was preparing me for what lay ahead.

My brother's death was my first experience with loss, and I

didn't like it. In the midst of the tragedy, I couldn't see anything good. Now, looking back, I see God was there . . . He was working in my life and the lives of so many . . . He was guiding my every step.

Over the next several years, I learned a lot about my big brother . . . what a righteous man of God he had become. His favorite hymn, "How Great Thou Art," was sung at his funeral. I learned he would open business meetings with prayer. A few short weeks before his death, I learned Jack had made amends, working to reconcile broken relationships in his life.

Jack's life was an example of how God can take an ordinary man and do extraordinary things in a willing life. I smile every time I think of seeing Jack again in the next life.

* * *

As Christians, we are not promised a life without trials and troubles. But we are promised the grace, peace, and strength to endure trials and troubles. Did Jack know he was going to die soon? I'm not sure, but today I believe the closer we are to God, the more we are prepared for anything that comes our way. Today I am grateful to have Jack's daughter, Tammy, and her family for being in my life. She is devout in her faith and is an inspiration to me.

BIRTH

Every cloud has a silver lining, and my silver lining in the midst of the storm of marital discord was the birth of my son in 1977. The first time I held him, I said, "Hi, I'm your mom." He already knew; I could swear he smiled at me. My son and I had bonded over the last nine months.

The sun rose and set on my son (and still does). I tried to be "supermom" to him, providing for all his needs, while in my own way, attempting to make up for my failures. My parenting skills always left room for improvement, having never been around children growing up. I never achieved any level of success at cooking or washing, but I always tried my best to be at every soccer game, karate lesson, and baseball tournament.

* * *

As I mature (chronologically and mentally), I've had years to reflect upon learning, growing, and changing. Funny how that learning, growing, and changing stuff never seems to stop.

DIVORCE

Becoming parents seemed to ease our marital conflicts for a while, but under pressure, old habits seemed to easily reappear. Emotional abuse, fear for our safety, and financial stress soon took its toll on me. Finally, in 1978, I had had enough.

I knew if my son was raised around violence, he would repeat that behavior. So the hardest decision for me was not whether to get a divorce but how to safely obtain a divorce. I was afraid for myself but doubly afraid for my son.

Rickey and I had a bitter separation and divorce, taking months to settle. It was nerve-wracking and emotionally exhausting. I sought sole custody of my son through the legal system, but the judge ruled against me. My parents supported me totally and were a much-needed shelter for us during the turbulence of these months. I've often wondered if my parents had not been there for me, what would have the outcome been? There are so many victims of domestic violence who have no one and nowhere to turn, so they continue to live in the midst of domestic abuse.

After the divorce, it was difficult for me to form a working relationship with Rickey. However, I knew it was necessary and best for our son. I think Rickey realized it, too.

* * *

Divorce, conflict, loss, resentment, bitterness . . . these are hard pills to swallow. Baby-step lessons were being learned on the importance of asking God's help when making decisions.

ANGER

Words said in haste, emotional wounds, those internal scars, can be far more crippling than physical injuries taking much longer to heal . . . if they ever do. Victims of violence of any kind often suffer lifelong consequences, physical as well as emotional. Therefore, to gauge the depth of the loss and the human tragedy, we must look farther than the loss of life and limb.

Researchers treating the victims of trauma report that how severely a person will suffer from a man-made trauma depends on the meaning the traumatic event holds for that person. A victim of trauma is robbed of the five basic emotional needs: safety, trust, control, esteem, and intimacy. Take away any of these, and scars start forming.

After my divorce, I was a ticking time bomb, angry at myself for having an abortion, angry at God for allowing these tragedies to occur and not bailing me out, and angry with anyone who happened to cross my path. I internalized most of my feelings for the sake of my son and immediate family, but that only increased my internal anger. In so doing, I was setting myself up for violent outbursts like the ones I had known growing up.

* * *

During this period, I can see God's timing was perfect, evidenced by the people He placed in my life just when I needed them. Healing began before I was aware, and it blossomed into something beautiful.

SUDDENLY SINGLE

Once my divorce was final, I was like a thoroughbred chomping at the bit to start the run at the Kentucky Derby. Trying to make up for lost time, having never experienced being single. When my son was away for the weekends, I went out with girl-friends. The carefree single life, having a good time, lost its luster after a year. I grew weary of living a dual life and didn't like the person I was becoming.

* * *

I was still wrestling for control of my life, but something was happening—I was being changed from the inside out.

GRANDMOTHER

In 1979, my beloved grandmother Bom passed away. My rock and safe harbor was now gone. This was an uncertain time. My foundation had been stripped away. I had so many questions. I remember telling myself I wasn't ready to stand on my own. As I recall, I believe I said the same thing when Daddy took my training wheels off my bicycle.

I began growing closer to my mother, caring for her more and more, just as she had taken care of her own mother. I started reading and writing and becoming more self-reflective. Some-where along the way, I started listening to a very still, small voice.

* * *

About this time, I began questioning my purpose on this earth. Surely I was born for a reason. Had I missed my opportunity to be what I was destined for?

CHAPTER 3
The Learning Years

Whoever loves discipline loves knowledge,
but he who hates reproof is stupid.
—PROVERBS 12:1

SINGLE PARENT

As I said before, a major blessing in my life in the midst of chaos was the birth of my son. Becoming a mother sparked a desire in me to be a better person. I wanted to do everything "right" for my baby. I had someone to take care of, to watch out for, to be accountable for. After my marriage failed, I turned all my attention to my son and being the best mother I could possibly be.

We enjoyed vacations, church camps, sports tournaments, and school activities. One Christmas Eve, I even awoke in the wee hours to drive to East Texas, buy a Bassett Hound puppy, and drive back to Dallas in time for work (puppy in hand), all to surprise my son that evening with his Christmas present. Freda (the puppy) was so cute . . . she was always tripping over her long ears in an effort to keep up with us!

I was a single parent for over a decade. I devoted all of my waking hours to my boy, while at the same time, taking care of both my parents in declining health and working way too many hours. Within a few years after the divorce, my son and I started attending church. For the longest time, I had avoided church for fear I would be singled out as the only person in the entire building who was alone. I felt like I was marked with a huge "D" stamped on my forehead. Where should I go to church? I went to the one place I knew and was comfortable—Cliff Temple. Attending week after week, I soon noticed a definite change in my spirits.

By 1983, my parents were aging and in declining health. Now divorced (again), Dad lived in an assisted living center while my mother, who had lost her sight due to macular degeneration, moved in with us. The three of us (Mom, my son, and I) moved all the way from Dallas to Duncanville (a whopping seven miles). Since Mom could no longer drive, I was now parenting one parent at home, parenting another parent in an assisted living center, parenting my son, working, paying my bills, paying my mother's bills, and looking for some "me" time (what time?!).

It was exhausting being caretaker for both parents and my son. Even with very full days and nights, I still longed for a family—one with a husband, wife, and children. I wanted a marriage that would last and a man I could respect, a good role model for my son. I would lay awake at night wondering what was going to happen to us after my parents were gone. I even tried praying for a family. "God, if you're up there, what's going to happen to us? Can you make us a family? Is there someone who could love my son as much as I do and be OK with a blind mother-in-law living with us?"

* * *

Why do we wait to pray as a last resort? Am I the only one who says, "Well, if all else fails, I'll pray"?

ANSWER TO PRAYER

I don't remember the exact date I prayed to God for a family, but I know within a few months, an answer arrived, and believe it or not, God does have a sense of humor. I had been single for eleven years, and I pretty much told God, "Lord, if you ever want me to get married again, you're going to have to bring someone to this church, because I just don't have time to go out and shop!"

In 1987, I was the single-adult director at church. I was always harping on my ministry partners to make visitors feel welcome—sit with them in church, invite them for lunch, you know. One Sunday, I received a call from one of the ministry partners that we'd had several visitors, and they (the partners) went out of their way to make them feel welcome.

The next Sunday, I was standing at the door of one of the single-adult classes, and in walks this guy with blonde hair and the most gorgeous blue eyes I had ever seen on a human being. And he winked . . . at me! I thought I had just died and gone to heaven! This was my lightning bolt! I later learned his name was Cary (like Cary Grant).

That same week, I was calling all the visitors to the singles class about a social we were having. I dialed the number, the phone rang, and a voice answered, "Cary Efurd." I said, "Is Cary Efurd there?" He said, "That's what I said, Cary Efurd." I said, "Did you say 'Cary Efurd?'" He said, "Is this a test?" We both laughed, and we still laugh to this day when we think about how we met.

A few weeks later, I had foot surgery (both feet). Cary visited me and brought his guitar, his miniature chess set, a homemade chocolate cake (that he baked), and the *Pittsburg* (Texas) *Ga-*

zette (all four pages of it). We talked for hours on end about every subject under the sun.

Over the course of the next few months, Cary would call me Monday, Tuesday, Wednesday, and Thursday nights at 10:30 p.m. sharp after he got home from night classes. When the phone rang, I would run to the phone like a giddy schoolgirl, wait until the third ring, then pick up the receiver leisurely (you can't let a guy know you're anxious). We would talk to the wee hours. He was my best friend then and still is my BFF and soul mate to this day. I love him to pieces.

Every Sunday during our "courtship," we would sit together in church, in the front pews, looking up at the choir. As time went on, we started holding hands, and then he started putting his arm around me. Choir members noticed the developing relationship before we even realized it ourselves. Our relationship was readily evident to all.

One Sunday, the singles Sunday school teacher asked everyone to tell about their most memorable New Year's Eve. Cary raised his hand immediately and told his New Year's story . . . how in 1984 he was physically hauled to the county jail in Pittsburg, Texas, in a straitjacket, then shipped to Terrell State Hospital for sixteen months for treatment for manic depression. He further explained what he had learned about himself and his disease, that he had been sober since 1985, and that he was proud to be a graduate of Terrell State (the hospital, that is).

Oh my! I can't tell you how many people started calling me that afternoon telling me I needed to back off and stop seeing this guy. I cooled my heels, backpedalled, and we stopped seeing each other for a couple of weeks. I don't know about Cary, but those weeks were completely miserable . . . it was as if a knife had ripped out my heart.

One evening, I was at home, reading my Bible, praying with my eyes open, confused about this "relationship thing," when I heard a voice behind me say, "Do you believe I can heal?" Now this wasn't a voice in my head; in fact, I actually turned around expecting to see someone behind me. I said, "God, if that's you, yes, I believe you can heal."

To make a long story short, Cary and I were married on November 12, 1988, having the fairy-tale wedding I had always wanted. We were surrounded by our children and all of our family and friends. God gave me that family I had prayed for.

* * *

I think every bride gets confused between a wedding and marriage. Weddings are fleeting, but marriage is a commitment. Commitment would prove to be a big lesson in my life.

BLENDING IN

With the divorce rate so high in America, blended families are now the norm rather than the exception. Fortunately, Cary and I were blessed to have three kids among us who got along well together. We enjoyed family trips and did everything in our power to make everyone feel like a family unit while still respecting their "other" families.

But there can still be conflict when blending "his, mine, and ours" together. Former conflict and resentments from previous marriages are only natural to bring into any new relationship. We definitely had our share of disputes and discord.

* * *

Many times I wanted to revert to my old family habit of "throwing in the towel," but was reminded (repeatedly) that commitment is worth any discomfort. God knew what He was doing when He brought Cary into my life.

PARENTING PARENTS

By 1992, both my mom and dad's health were failing dramatically. My dad continued to grow weaker from a slow-growing non-Hodgkin lymphoma immune disorder (Waldenstrom macroglobulinemia). Due to his already weakened condition, a near-fatal car accident left him immobilized, his legs quickly atrophying to the point he could no longer walk. He was moved to a nursing home for physical therapy, but we soon realized Dad would be bound to a wheelchair the rest of his life. Eventually, we moved him to a nursing home closer to Duncanville.

A few months later, my mother developed heart problems and suffered a mild stroke. After undergoing surgery for blocked arteries, the strain on her already weakened heart pushed her into heart failure. From one facility to the next, Mom's health deteriorated to the point hospice became necessary.

For over a year, I would leave work, stop by the nursing home, go home, check on Mom, then do the necessary household chores (cooking, shopping, paying bills, laundry, school activities, and sometimes, sleeping). I was stressed and stretched to the max. I thought I was the only one affected by the stress, but the ensuing family arguments proved that this time was stressful for everyone.

In 1993, the doctor told us Mom had a few months left. We set up hospice in our home. In November of that year, the hospice nurse called me at work to say, "Your mom will pass soon." She explained Mother had been talking to the "others" in the room, telling them she would be joining them. That night, I was letting go of my mom, crying out to God asking him to take Momma home and end her suffering. The next day, preparing for the inevitable, I moved to Mom's room and lay down on the couch by her bed. I never closed my eyes, but suddenly, I sat up, just in time to see Momma take her last breath on this earth. It was "not of this world" —I could sense her spirit leave her body. She was now at peace. That was November 3, 1993.

In late December, just six weeks later, my dad was admitted to the hospital for pneumonia, a result of his weakened immune system. On January 4, 1994, Daddy passed away. I had lost both my parents within nine weeks' time.

The loss of Mom and Dad within such a short period was overwhelming. I never had time to grieve for one parent before facing the loss of the other. It was after both funerals that I realized I no longer had a "home" to run to. I was now the "matriarch" of my family, and I didn't have a clue what that meant or how to be a matriarch. It was time for me to get my house in order.

I have many memories of my parents. One of the memories I cherish the most is Mother praying at the dinner table. Even at the end of her life, suffering from a level of dementia, she would say grace so eloquently:

> Our Gracious Heavenly Father, we thank Thee this day for the rich abundance with which Thou hast blessed us. We humbly ask Thee to bless this food to our nourishment, and our bodies to Your service. Amen.

However tragic 1993 and 1994 were in the loss of my parents, they were mere stepping stones preparing me for trials yet to come.

* * *

Every time I hear "Cat's in the Cradle,"[1] *I recall all the times I removed myself from family. At some point it becomes too late to retrieve lost opportunities. I regret not having those memories . . .*

---

[1] Harry Chapin, "Cat's in the Cradle," on *Verities and Balderdash*, Elektra Records, 1974.

so embrace every moment you have your family with you.

SISTER

My half-sister, Betty, was twenty years old when I was born. She was already married with a family of her own before I appeared on the scene. I never got a chance to know her until my dad became ill. At that point, I connected with a family I never knew.

Betty and I were never close . . . distanced by age, location, and family dynamics . . . but we shared the same DNA, nuances, and the same way of handling relationships and conflict that our dad did. Betty answered a lot of questions for me about my dad and helped provide closure to those questions.

I admire Betty because she was the "glue" that held her family together. She was a marvelous example of a matriarch.

SCHOOL

After my parents passed away, I went back to school to finish my degree (finally). A thirty-year degree plan is better than none at all. It took three grueling years, attending weekends and nights, but I did it. I graduated in 1996 cum laude from Dallas Baptist University with a counseling degree. Accomplishing that single goal made me feel better about myself. It gave me courage to push on.

* * *

I chose counseling as a career path after my brother was killed. Although there were detours along the way, and although I never pursued a full-time counseling career, counseling has been useful in every area of my life.

THE NIGHT

When I married Cary, I had only heard the term "manic depression" (bipolar disorder) in passing. I thought it was like a thyroid problem: you pop a pill and everything's A-OK.

It happens slowly over a period of time. First you get busy and forget to take your medicine; then you're trying to keep your business going, so you don't sleep as much as you should; then, because you're busy and you're not sleeping, you're not eating right and drinking too much caffeine.

Then you have the bills to worry about, payroll, and the challenge of keeping business coming in the door. To top it off, you have a wife who up and quits work, thinking she's going to "help" get this business shaped up.

Now you have no income, except for what you pull in, and a wife who is not working and depending on you for support. You have mounting debt to keep the business going, and pretty soon, you don't have a pot to . . . plant petunias in.

In 1995, the house next door to us burned to the ground. Cary and I were able to buy the lot for a song. We thought we would rebuild and "flip" it quickly to get out of debt. That was our plan, but our plans didn't work out the way we envisioned, so we ended up with a lot more debt than we started with.

Cary and I sold both our house and the house next door, barely making enough to pay off some debt, but not all. We downsized from 3,000 square feet to a 600-square-foot condo.

Then the motor on my car burned up, and we didn't have money to buy a car, so we leased a company vehicle. This would give me transportation to the new job I had just started to help make ends meet.

October 1, 1997. I arrived home from work. As soon as I walked in the door, I knew something was wrong. Cary had rearranged all the furniture, and there were sticky notes everywhere. Then he left in my (leased) Jeep, saying he would be back in a little while.

The phone call came later that night. Cary was at Parkland Hospital. He said he had had a wreck but that everything would be all right. I remember his speech was loud, quick, and pressured. I called one of our employees to take me to Parkland.

As soon as the police report was available, I learned the full extent of the tragedy that happened on October 1, 1997, the night that changed so many lives. The next day, a young man of eighteen passed away, leaving a seventeen-year-old wife and an eight-month-old baby boy.

The accident occurred as a result of Cary's manic episode. While speeding, he rear-ended a vehicle stopped at a red light, locking bumpers and flipping both vehicles in the air. Our Jeep, the one Cary was driving, landed on its right side. As Cary climbed out of the wreckage, the other Jeep he hit burst into flames, trapping the driver in the front seat.

Cary leaped out of our car and ran to the other Jeep. Despite many bystanders, Cary didn't hesitate and reached into the fire to pull the driver out of the burning wreckage. In his mania, Cary was oblivious to pain yet hyper-sensitive to his surroundings. Cary carried the young driver, still on fire, to a grassy sidewalk, staying by his side until paramedics arrived. This young man of eighteen looked up at Cary and asked him to tell his wife and child he loved them. Cary said he would. We don't know for sure, but that may have been the last words this young man ever spoke. The victim had third-degree burns over 75 percent of his body. Cary had second- and third-degree burns on his hands and arms.

Although the Jeep that Cary hit was a total loss, by some miracle, the only item untouched in the blaze was the Bible in the front passenger seat. Fortunately, being oblivious to pain and the danger of the fire due to his mania, Cary showed no hesitancy in going into the flames and pulling the victim from the burning wreckage. To this day the victim's handprints are etched into Cary's forearms.

The trauma of October 1, 1997, pushed Cary into an acute hyper-manic state. After arriving at Parkland, he broke a nurse's nose, ripped a toilet and sink out of the bathroom, had to be restrained by four men, and received multiple doses of tranquilizers before he could be sedated.

It didn't take long before reporters and personal injury investigators started calling. Within a week of the accident, Cary and I were sued in a personal injury lawsuit against our business and us personally. Cary was charged with criminal negligent homicide and also faced assault charges from a hospital nurse. He was sent from Parkland to Timberlawn and finally wound up in Terrell State Mental Hospital for thirty days. I had a job I was trying to keep, a business I had no hope of running, no money, mounting debt, and no car to run away in.

Family members pitched in, lending support and providing a car to drive. We hired three sets of lawyers for the civil, criminal, and bankruptcy actions working against us simultaneously. I was now working my day job, an evening job, and was looking for a weekend job.

To say I was angry at life was putting it mildly. I was mad and bitter at everyone and everything . . . my circumstances, Cary, and God. Why us, Lord? Why *me*, Lord? I saw myself in a small 600-foot prison we called home feeling like a trapped animal. I was not a pleasant person to be around.

I wanted to run away as hard and fast as my car would travel. I wanted to bury my head under the covers and come out of hiding when it was all over. But something inside me caused me to take pause. I couldn't leave . . . we had children, family, friends, and people we didn't even know looking at us, watching our every move. Instead of choosing the easier road, I chose the higher path to honor commitment, being the "matriarch" our children needed, however imperfect a matriarch I was.

Healing in our relationship and family began gradually. It started with many tears; the trial; letters to the victim's family; restitution; setting up a trust for the victim's son; paying back bankruptcy debt we didn't legally owe, but was God's way; working hard; praying; attending Bible study; and surrounding ourselves with people who prayed for us and with us.

I can't say at what point the turnaround in me happened, but my perceived "prison" eventually turned into a "sanctuary" where I was meeting Jesus for the first time, up close and personal. I no longer had all the trappings of worldly "possessions" distracting me and soon began losing interest in what the world thought of me.

For the first time in my life, I didn't base my decisions on my emotions. Don't get me wrong: I still wasn't sure how I felt about Cary. At the moment I didn't like him . . . I wasn't even sure if I still loved him . . . but I didn't leave him, choosing instead to honor the commitment that we had made in 1988, "in sickness and in health." I acted on the decision, and the feelings eventually followed.

So many unexplained "God things" happened: the Bible that didn't burn up; the handprints on Cary's forearms that should have long ago faded but are still readily visible; the attorney friend who suddenly appeared in bankruptcy court, shortening our court appearance once she asked the judge if she could "hug the debtor" (the attorney whom we haven't seen since); the man who showed up out of nowhere after Cary prayed for someone to "buy our little business"; the employees who were loyal to us to the bitter end; the job that suddenly became available when Cary needed a job; the GAP insurance I didn't know we had on our leased Jeep that paid off that debt; the job opportunities that came my way that provided the income to get by; all the miracles that you become aware of once your blinders are removed.

Cary and I both, to this day, remember that time as our wake-up call and are grateful to God for it, not for the tragic loss of a young man's life, but for the cleansing and renewal we both experienced, which continues to this day.

It took about two years before Cary and I started seeing some "light" in our relationship and our lives. Little by little, day by day, we grew stronger, deeper in our walk, and we both believe that sharing our testimony of that experience was a key component in deepening our faith.

During some tumultuous times, I viewed our residence as a prison. Six months later, I perceived it as a sanctuary. That change in perspective gave me sanity, peace, and increased faith to weather all the storms in my life.

I imagine shepherd-turned-king David[2] had a change of perspective a few times in his life, too. As a teenager he was entrusted with the care of the family flocks. He was the sole line of defense between a lion or a bear and his family's livelihood. David didn't shrink from responsibility and retreat, but he very well may have said to those predators, "You are going to die some way and some day, and I'm here to make sure you die this way and today." With each encounter, David increased his faith.

Years later, David met another predator . . . Goliath. As the Israelites cowered with fear, telling David that Goliath was too big to hurt, David's perspective was different. Shepherd-soon-to-be-king David ran quickly to confront Goliath thinking, "He's too big to miss."

* * *

Looking back to that time in our lives, Cary and I find comfort believing the victim of the accident was a believer. To this day I

---

[2] See 1 Samuel:16-21, the Holy Bible.

watch Cary quietly looking at and rubbing his forearms where the handprints of that young man are indelibly imprinted—a constant reminder of the storms in our lives and the One who brought healing—Jesus Christ.

CHAPTER 4
The Restoration Years

*Then again He laid His hands on his eyes; and he looked
intently and was restored, and began to see everything clearly.*
–MARK 8:25

FORGIVENESS

It is said one of the constants in life is change. Circumstances change from moment to moment. People come in and out of our lives in an instant. Likewise, God allows trials in our lives to "peel us like an onion," and we end up being transformed.

Cary and I witnessed change in our own lives. We sought to forgive and to be forgiven. We wanted to make peace with our past.

Years later, after we started a business, celebrated graduations, endured job losses, and attended college and weddings, Cary and I received a call that my ex-husband, Rickey, was in the Veterans Administration hospital in Dallas. Rickey had just received a diagnosis of stage IV terminal cancer. Our son asked if Cary and I could find a pastor to go speak to his father.

We immediately set out on our mission to find a minister to speak with Rickey. We asked pastors at two churches and two separate ministries, but for one reason or another, had no success. So my husband, Cary, decided to visit my ex-husband, Rickey, himself. After all, he and Rickey had a common bond— me and our son. Over the course of a few weeks, Cary spent time with Rickey every day, bought him a Bible, prayed with him, read him Scripture, explained the Good News, and eventually led him to a renewed faith in Christ. Within weeks Rickey was using that same Bible to share his renewed faith with other patients at the hospital.

The cancer spread quickly. Within no time it was apparent the end of Rickey's earthly life was coming to a close. That remaining time allowed me to make much-needed amends with Rickey for the hurt we had shared. For that I am grateful. One night Cary and I received a call that Rickey was in ICU. We rushed to the hospital to say our goodbyes.

Cary gave the eulogy at Rickey's funeral. Let me repeat that . . . my husband gave the eulogy at my ex-husband's funeral. How does that happen? That's not something that happens naturally. Love won out.

That simple, selfless act eased the remorse of a dying man.

That simple, selfless act gave an earthly father to a fatherless son.

That simple, selfless act fast-tracked a healing process in our lives.

That simple, selfless act sparked a desire, a yearning deep inside both Cary and me, to be more like Him.

The next few years brought spiritual growth to both of us. We committed ourselves to work in various ministries, started tithing for the first time in our marriage, and devoted more time to prayer and Bible study. We witnessed growth for the good in us personally, professionally, and materially. I guess you could say once we started "eating the right spiritual diet," you could see the rewards.

I was learning many lessons about being transparent in my own life, and I was coming to terms with the part I played in the decisions in my life. Instead of pretending events and decisions never happened, sweeping them under the rug, pretending someone else was to blame, I began taking ownership of them and readily admitting I had responsibility in and for them.

But . . .

I was still holding onto one part of my life I thought was impossible for even God to heal—my "secret."

PART II

SURRENDER IT!

Either your faith will kill your secrecy,
or your secrecy will kill your faith.
—Dr. Robert Jeffress
senior pastor, First Baptist Church of Dallas,
from "The Other Side of Election"
sermon, September 21, 2014

CHAPTER 5
Surrender

And if I give all my possessions to feed the poor, and if I
surrender my body to be burned,
but do not have love, it profits me nothing.
−1 Corinthians 13:3

By the time the new century (Y2k) rolled around, science was revealing more and more truths about life inside the womb. Technology had progressed to the point you could "see," through sonogram technology, a child develop, smile, hiccup, and respond to stimulus. This new technology was fascinating, and the research behind it triggered memories I thought I had buried long ago. Science was revealing what I instinctively had known all along . . . that my abortion did have consequences . . . that it was a baby, not a clump of cells as I'd been told, that died that day in June 1973. Guilt and regret once again engulfed me. I couldn't forgive myself for what I had done in 1973, so I naturally concluded it was inconceivable that a Holy God could possibly forgive a sin as horrendous as killing my own baby.

For decades I had held on and protected my "secret" so much that it changed me. I isolated myself, fearing someone would look into my eyes and "find me out." That secret made it even more difficult to have a deep relationship with my God. As a result, depression set in, my behavior changed, and I looked for any means to soothe my troubled soul.

I put up a good front. To others I looked like I had it all together, but on the inside? Well, that was another matter altogether. I pushed bad memories down so deep I thought they were buried forever. I erased years from memory. But God had a different plan for me. By allowing situations and people to enter my life, I began to move toward Him.

By 2008, Cary and I had grown stagnant in our worship. We longed for a reignition of our spiritual engines and began looking for a new church home. We wanted a church that was not afraid to preach the Gospel. We began attending First Baptist Church of Dallas. Once we joined First Dallas, we plugged into the ministries of the church, formed relationships, and increased our stewardship immediately. This had a positive ripple effect into every part of our lives.

In 2010 I developed some health issues. For years doctors could not diagnose the cause of various symptoms I was experiencing, but I continued to have infection after infection. I was scheduled for sinus surgery in late 2010, but an immune study required by my doctor before any surgical procedure came back very low. He immediately cancelled the surgery and referred me to a specialist. Miraculously, the infectious disease specialist diagnosed me with a primary immune disorder, common variable immune disease (CVID). Once the diagnosis was determined, the treatment was simple—monthly infusions of gamma globulin. It is a hereditary disorder, similar to the Waldenstrom's macroglobulinemia my dad had, which eventually contributed to his death. However, my diagnosis, CVID, is not life-threatening. Paying no attention to what the doctors were telling me, in my mind, I thought my days were numbered. For whatever reason, my immune disorder spurred me to take action on some much-needed spiritual housework.

I love to sing and have been in choir my entire life, from kindergarten on up. The Sanctuary Choir at First Dallas was one of the first ministries I joined at church. The music ministry became a second family to me. We would practice together, laugh together, and cry together. Sitting in choir week after week, I witnessed peace on the faces of other choir members. I heard joy in their voices. I listened to transforming testimonies of what God did in their lives. Whatever they had, I knew I wanted.

Then one Sunday evening, the pastor spoke on forgiveness. The choir sang:

> All to Jesus I surrender;
> all to Him I freely give;
> I will ever love and trust Him,
> in His presence daily live.
>
> I surrender all, I surrender all,
> all to thee, my blessed Savior,
> I surrender all.[3]

Suddenly it struck me. I couldn't sing. I could barely stand up. I was motionless. I heard a still, small whisper in my ear. "Debby, are you sure? Have you really surrendered everything to me?" I had reached my breaking point. I thought, "Lord, I can't go on like this anymore. Please help me."

Following the service, I rushed quickly out of church to the seclusion of the car in the parking garage. I didn't want anyone to see me crying. Once there, I broke down. It was at that point the dam holding back thirty-eight years of tears broke. I was

---

[3] Judson W. Van DeVenter and W. S. Weeden, "I Surrender All," 1896.

holding onto God for dear life. It was at that point I surrendered and stopped running.

A few weeks went by and I inquired about volunteering at the Downtown Pregnancy Center,[4] a mission of First Baptist Church of Dallas. For years I had been drawn to help young mothers in a crisis pregnancy. I wanted to tell them not to repeat my experience. When I arrived at the center, I met a woman I had known from my Oak Cliff days. We reconnected instantly, recalling fond memories of our favorite neighborhood and cafe. She gave me a tour of the center as we promised to meet for lunch the following week.

I enjoyed my time with Vicki and was eager to get involved with the center. Although I had never admitted my abortion to anyone other than my husband, I felt at ease with Vicki, and without hesitation, told her of my own abortion. Over lunch Vicki explained that all post-abortive volunteers are required to go through post-abortive healing. Post-abortive? What was that? This was all new to me. I didn't know what she was talking about, had never heard the term "post abortive,"[5] and wasn't sure "post abortive" applied to me at all. After a few minutes, though, I learned something new—that I was post-abortive, and that, in fact, I would probably be a good candidate as the poster child for "post abortion."

Now this is where it gets interesting. In order to volunteer at the center, I knew I had to go through post-abortion recovery because that's a requirement of the center. I had no clue what I

[4] Involved for Life, Inc. comprises the collective ministries of the Downtown Pregnancy Center, the Uptown Women's Center, and Sonograms on Site in Dallas, Texas.

[5] "Post abortive" is a term first used by Vincent Rue, PhD, an American psychotherapist who has published and coauthored a number of studies finding that abortion increases women's risk of mental health problems. The studies, as well as the issue of abortion, continue to be the subject of much debate.

was signing up for, but I didn't hesitate, saying, "*Yes!* Sign me up." Actually, I didn't think I needed a recovery group at all, but if that's what it took to be a volunteer, I'd do it. Within a week, an opening became available for an upcoming group starting in a few weeks. (Believe me when I say, after working in post-abortion ministry for several years, I guarantee this is *not* the norm.)

I did everything in my power to get out of going to that recovery Bible study. I told myself I didn't need help, that the requirements of attending were silly, that I was healed and didn't need extra "healing," that this group was for everyone else, not for me. But I went. I walked into that group a rebellious, helpless, hopeless, and angry woman, and I walked out after three days with peace, hope, and forgiveness. I was finally free of the baggage I'd been pulling behind me all my life. For the first time in thirty-five years, I could breathe freely and was able to accept God's gift that had been waiting for me, still wrapped up in a beautiful package with a bow, all those years. I had never accepted that gift of forgiveness. I knew in my heart my first son, whom I named Aden, and I would one day meet: that I would hold him and tell him how much I loved him. But until that day, I knew where he was and that he was safe. The Bible says, "[A]nd you will know the truth and the truth will set you free" (John 8:32). Now I understood what that meant.

Thinking back, I see more clearly how decisions we make in our lives often have repercussions not only for us but also for others as well. From the day I drove home from that abortion clinic, I closed myself off from others, put on my happy face, and tried to forget what I'd done. I hid behind walls of shame and guilt that grew higher and thicker year after year. I didn't allow myself to feel anything, not crying or laughing, for a very long time. I didn't realize then that unresolved grief can cause such internal trauma. I was running away, hiding from God, the world, and myself because I thought my problem was too big for God to handle.

But no matter how far or fast I ran from the truth, God never left me. He kept pursuing me until I fell in a pit so deep that the only direction I could reach was up to my God in heaven. It was at that point in 2011 that I surrendered, stopped running, saw my need, and sought recovery. That's when real recovery took place, and restoration continues to this day.

God orchestrated situations and people to enter into my life, and I began to move toward Him. Gradually, I was being peeled like an onion . . . layer by layer . . . of years of shame, regret, anger, and resentment, until one day I sought more of Jesus than I did of me. The day I felt closest to my God is when I confessed my deepest, darkest secret . . . for me, it was my secret of abortion. For you, it may be something else equally deep, dark, and secretive. It was in that hour of public confession, when, for once, I was more concerned with that one person in the congregation who needed to hear they were not alone in their silent suffering than I was for myself, that I was closest to God. I walked through my greatest fear and found victory. I can truthfully say that confession was good for this weary soul.

Secrecy and isolation are killers, allowing a person to get away with pretty much anything they want while rationalizing their every behavior and justifying their actions. Given the foothold of secrecy and isolation, addictions easily take hold and then increase to the point where they consume mind, body, and soul.

CHAPTER 6
The Next Year

Cease striving and know that I am God; I will be exalted
among the nations, I will be exalted in the earth.
–PSALM 46:10

It would be a year before I would share my story publicly.
In that year, God prepared me in ways that deepened my faith,
increased my joy, and strengthened my platform for the future.

Little by little, I was becoming more intentional in my faith.
I found more and more freedom to speak openly and share my
faith. Yet I still had not publicly shared my abortion experience.
The problem with secrets is that no matter who holds them,
they are destructive. Full intimacy is impossible when secrets
are kept. Secrets are fertile ground for future trouble.

The opportunity to share my story publicly was approaching.
I knew it would happen; I just didn't know when that opportunity would occur.

CHAPTER 7

The Turning Point

For we walk by faith, not by sight.
–2 CORINTHIANS 5:7

The opportunity to publicly share my story occurred on Palm Sunday 2012. Weeks prior to the service, choir members were asked to volunteer by giving cardboard testimonies at the upcoming Palm Sunday service. I was one of the first to volunteer, my arm shooting up like a rocket. I don't know why . . . it was a reflex . . . and I surprised myself at my reaction. Now that I had volunteered, I wasn't sure what I wanted to say on my card.

My first attempt at writing my card was "Forgiven and set free after thirty-five years." Well, that didn't tell you very much, did it? Forgiven and set free from what? I knew all along what God wanted me to say, but I was still resistant to revealing my secret.

I was afraid of what others would think of me (the same old story: expecting a different result). Finally, I decided on what the card should say: "Burdened by the guilt of abortion for thirty-five years. At last forgiven and set free from that guilt." There, I *said* it.

The night of the service, the sanctuary was packed. There were twenty-five of us giving our testimonies. For weeks God had been preparing me for this moment, and I was growing stronger in my faith and resolve in hopes that at least one person in the congregation would receive encouragement from my little testimony.

Several months after the Palm Sunday service, I received a call from Dr. Doran Bugg, the minister of music at First Baptist Church of Dallas. He said, "Debby, do you believe in the power of a personal testimony?" I said, "Absolutely. In fact, I think it's often more effective than sermons." He told me he was glad I thought so because the music and media ministries were partnering for a special concert in August and wanted to highlight my testimony in video during the service. Would I be willing to do that? I may have hesitated one or two seconds before saying, "YES!"

But there was one person I needed to meet and talk to personally before I gave my testimony. The one person I dreaded facing for fear of what he would think of me. The one person whose love I was afraid of losing—my son. For years I avoided telling him what his mother had done, projecting every possible scenario that could occur. I imagined he would tell me to get out of his life. I imagined he would ask me how I could have done such a thing. I imagined he would tell me I could never see my grandchildren again. But none of that happened. I told him the truth about what happened in June 1973, and I was met with more love, grace, and warmth than I deserved. My son was showing his mother that love does win out. It was an amazing moment.

Preparations for the upcoming RISE concert began immediately. Rehearsals were conducted over six weeks. I was sequestered for the filming of the video testimony over several weeks. Until the dress rehearsal, no one in the choir or orchestra knew who was giving the testimony that would be shown. With permission, I addressed the choir and orchestra before the rehearsal to thank them in advance for their love and support and dedicating the results of our collective effort to the glory of God.

On August 26, 2012, the RISE concert was held for a capacity crowd at First Baptist Church of Dallas. That night, something amazing happened. Even with an overflow crowd in attendance, I wasn't nervous. I was more concerned with the one who needed to hear what I said than I was about myself. I felt empowered and encouraged in sharing. Can't explain it, don't know how it works, but ever since that night in 2012, it happens time after time after time I share my deepest hurt and the resulting victory.

* * *

And they overcame him because of the blood of the Lamb and because of the word of their testimony, and they did not love their life even when faced with death.
–REVELATION 12:11

CHAPTER 8
Who, Me?

*The fear of the LORD is the beginning of wisdom, and the
knowledge of the Holy One is understanding.*
−PROVERBS 9:10

Soon after the RISE concert, I was asked to lead post-abortion support, facilitating abortion-recovery Bible studies for clients at Involved for Life, one of the missions of the First Baptist Church of Dallas. This was a tremendous opportunity for me and proved to be an invaluable training ground. The collaborative efforts of Involved for Life's leadership allowed me to easily transition into my new role.

My experience with Involved for Life proved to be my "graduate studies" for ministry, and I learned volumes about abortion-recovery ministry very quickly. There was a great deal to learn because the issues surrounding abortion and the post-abortive community, as well as the problems caused by abortion, are enormous and profound. Current statistics show one in three women in any setting have an abortion in their past, and close to 80 percent of those women exhibit symptoms of post-abortion stress.[6]

With the help of my friend Kim from Involved for Life, we set about holding our first recovery Bible study group. Thanks to her caring spirit and planning skills, we guided several women through the grief process during our nine weeks together.

Over the course of several months, more recovery groups were held. I would counsel women one-on-one, in person or by phone, women whose lives had been turned topsy-turvy by abortion. It was gut-wrenching to hear their hurt, a reminder of the hurt we shared, yet rewarding when I could share my experience of hope and restoration.

But on a much broader scale, there was a legislative battle brewing in Texas over abortion rights. In the summer of 2013, battle lines had been drawn in Austin, Texas. National and international attention were now focused on a pro-life bill to ban abortions in the state of Texas after twenty weeks of pregnancy and hold abortion facilities accountable for obeying health and safety laws. Hearings saw halls packed with thousands wanting to testify both for and against the bill.

The call for volunteers went out from Operation Outcry,[7] and I responded immediately. I was briefed on the *who, what,*

---

[6] Post-abortion stress (PAS) is a subset of post-traumatic stress disorder (PTSD) and is a reaction to an abortion. Initially, some experience relief, but over time, many experience deeper emotions, such as grief, shame, depression, crying, guilt, anger, and regret. Nightmares, flashbacks to the abortion, lowered self-esteem, problems with intimacy, or substance abuse are not uncommon. The intensity of post-abortion stress varies from sadness to suicidal feelings. According to a survey released by the Elliot Institute (originally published in Post-Abortion Review, 2 (3): 4-8, Fall 1994), 90 percent of women regret having had an abortion, 70 percent rated their emotional aftereffects as severe, 87 percent now believe abortion was the wrong choice, and 61 percent believe that their abortion made their life worse.

[7] Operation Outcry is the ministry of the Justice Foundation to end the pain of abortion by exposing the truth about its devastating impact on women, men, and families. The Justice Foundation seeks to protect the fundamental freedoms and rights essential to the preservation of American society. The Foundation represents clients free of charge in cases in the areas of limited government, free markets, private property, parental school choice, parental rights in education, and enforcing laws to protect women's health.

when and *where* (I already knew the *why*), and with statement in hand, I set out in the pre-dawn hours to drive from Dallas to Austin. It was Monday, July 1, and all eyes were watching Austin as the Texas State Legislature was set to open a second special session to decide the fate of a pro-life bill that had failed the previous week due to a last-minute filibuster. I arrived in Austin at 10:00 a.m.

I had seen media coverage and heard stories about the thousands of protesters in Austin, but nothing prepared me for what I saw as I walked to the steps of the state Capitol. Orange (pro-choice) and blue (pro-life) shirts were everywhere, pouring in from every direction. With assistance from the Texas Department of Public Safety, I was able to get into the Capitol without delay, but the Capitol rotunda was filling fast.

At 11:30 a.m., the Operation Outcry press conference started. Nine brave women gave statements of how their abortions had hurt them. At the conclusion of the press conference, there was not a dry eye in the briefing room.

Afterwards, our nine-member entourage was escorted by Texas Department of Public Safety troopers to the Capitol rotunda. Screams from the thousands present inside the Capitol nearly ripped the roof off. With the crowds in the rotunda, maneuvering was difficult. Shouting, chanting, jeering, heckling . . . the sound was deafening. DPS troopers were stationed on each floor to maintain order, arresting those out of control. Suddenly, a groundswell of the melody "Amazing Grace"[8] softly grew from one floor to the next, gaining in volume and power as it rose from floor to floor, until the melody of that old hymn quieted the protests.

The request and response for testimonies from women hurt

---

[8] John Newton, "Amazing Grace," in *Olney Hymns,* (Olney, Buckinghamshire, UK: n.p., 1779), 53.

by abortion was overwhelming. It eventually helped turn the tide in the state Capitol. But Austin was just one battle in a much bigger war. In the years ahead, much more help will be needed—more testimonies, greater physical presence in House and Senate chambers, and more calls to state and national representatives.

It's apparent the line in the sand had been drawn in Austin, the Alamo of the twenty-first century. At last people were hearing the truth about abortion in ways previously unimagined. Change is occurring in other states as well. National attention to pro-life issues is growing . . . main-stream media is suddenly saying, "Wait a minute—maybe there is something to this life begins at conception thing." US legislation on abortion is once again being considered, and judicial cases may one day be heard by the US Supreme Court to hopefully overturn *Roe v. Wade.*

While the battle was raging in Austin, media was camped out in Austin. TV and media reports were given every few minutes. Here is one example of national reporting:

(Reuters)[9] Thousands of opponents of a Texas proposal to tighten abortion restrictions rallied outside the statehouse on Monday, giving a hero's welcome to Democratic state Senator Wendy Davis, whose 11-hour speech stalled the measure last week.

As the Republican-dominated state legislature convened for a second special session on Monday, supporters said they expected the bill would pass this time. With few exceptions, it would ban abortions after 20 weeks of pregnancy.

The proposal would also subject abortion clinics to stron-

[9] Corrie MacLaggin, "Opponents of Texas abortion restrictions rally at Capitol," Reuters (US), July 1, 2013.

ger health and safety rules, which the nation's biggest abortion provider, Planned Parenthood, has said could cause all but six of Texas' 42 abortion centers to close. Republicans have called that an exaggeration.

"A great number of us have felt discouraged about the current state of affairs here," Davis told the rally as she stood before a huge Texas flag. "Some of us have felt mad. Today is different, though. Don't you feel it? We feel hope."

While Democrats have said they may try new delaying tactics, they have given no details, and they are unlikely to be able to filibuster the bill again during the session.

The crowd, many carrying umbrellas for protection from the sun, listened to live music by Natalie Maines of the Dixie Chicks and carried signs that said things like, "Wendy for governor," and "Separate your church from my uterus."

The political battle in Texas is the latest in a national debate over abortion restrictions. While a dozen states have restricted late-term abortions, Arkansas has banned abortions after 12 weeks and North Dakota as early as six weeks.

Inside the Texas Capitol on Monday, supporters of the measure sang "Amazing Grace" and held a press conference featuring women who said they regretted having abortions. Molly White of Belton, Texas, spoke of how her two abortions caused damage to her cervix and a lifetime of emotional pain.

Texas Governor Rick Perry, a Republican who sets the agenda for special sessions of the Legislature, called lawmakers back to Austin after Davis staged a filibuster to block the abortion bill in the final day of the first special session.

Republicans managed to stop her talking and voted to pass the bill, but hundreds of bill opponents screamed from the gallery as senators were voting. The disruption helped delay Lieutenant Governor David Dewhurst signing the bill and sending it to the governor on time.

If the bill passes, Texas would become the 13th U.S. state to pass a 20-week ban.

"It seems as close to a sure thing as you can get," said Jonathan Saenz, president of Texas Values, an advocacy group that supports the proposal. But he added, "As we saw during the first special session, until it's completely done and the process is finished, there are no guarantees. That's going to motivate both sides to do everything they can to ensure victory."

On Monday, the state House and Senate each referred the bill to committees, and the House panel was set to meet on Tuesday to consider the measure. The full House and Senate are not scheduled to meet again until July 9.

Special sessions can last up to 30 days. The Texas Legislature typically meets every other year for 140 days, and lawmakers wrapped up their regular session on May 27. Perry called lawmakers back for the first special session that same day, but he did not add abortion legislation to the agenda until June 11. This time, abortion is already on the agenda.

Perry assured attendees at the National Right to Life convention in Dallas last week that the measure would pass this time.

"This is a hard fight," state Senator Kirk Watson, a Democrat, said at the rally. "There will be setbacks, but there isn't anything more important."

Yes, the Austin experience made a profound impact on me—it's hard to express in words. After the press conference, men and women approached me, grateful for my willingness to be their "voice" after having lost their own "voice" to abortion. Parents asked me to pray for their daughters whose lives had been ripped apart following their abortion. Students pleaded with me to come speak on campus . . . they had no one to stand up for life; they referred to the campus as a "death mill."

But it was the overwhelming surging emotion and size of the crowds that made my heart ache. I witnessed a level of anger and mayhem that is unfathomable. Busloads of protesters were arriving from across the country, carrying signs either in support of easy access to abortion or signs to protect the rights of the unborn. My thoughts kept returning to Colonel William Barrett Travis drawing his famous "line in the sand" at the Battle of the Alamo.

As I drove back to Dallas the evening of July 1, I was exhausted, mentally and physically. Trying to sort through the emotions of the day, I remember saying, "Lord, I don't understand. What do *You* want me to do? What can one person do to be salt and light in the midst of so much darkness? Abortion has created the largest demographic in our culture."

CHAPTER 9
An Enormous Giant

He inquired of the Lord for him, gave him provisions, and
gave him the sword of Goliath the Philistine.
–1 SAMUEL 22:10

Before I go any further, I want to explain what I mean when I talk about the "enormity" of abortion in our country and the issues surrounding the post-abortive demographic. So I think it best that we pause for an educational moment.

Since 1973, a new mission field of the "walking wounded" has been created in this country and exists throughout the world. What are we talking about? Those who have experienced the pain of abortion. We call them the walking wounded because they so often carry physical, mental, and emotional trauma with them for years, many carrying their secret to their grave. Wounded people wound others. That's what abortion does. There are no winners in abortion. It's about a mother, a father, and a child. The child loses his or her life, and afterwards, the parents suffer emotionally, spiritually, and often, physically. If we allow the issue of abortion to remain solely in the political realm, we remove the humanity of life from the holocaust of abortion.

You may be saying to yourself, "Well that's all well and good, Debby, but what does that have to do with me?" It has everything to do with you and me. Let me share some statistics:[10]

- Abortion is currently one of the most common surgical procedures in the US.
- It is the leading cause of death (heart disease kills 600,000 annually, while over 1.2 million pre-born children die per year as a result of abortion).
- Three in ten women in America are post-abortive by the time they are forty-five. This implies that around 30 percent of men are also post-abortive.
- Abortion is an enormous industry, generating more than $800 million each year for abortion doctors, facilities, and providers.[11]
- Since 1973, over 57 million abortions are estimated to have occurred in the US.
- Research shows 80 percent of women having an abortion suffer varying degrees of post-abortion stress (a subset of post-traumatic stress disorder, as it relates to abortion); 20 percent of those experience symptoms that are life-altering (including a four times higher risk of suicide and a two times higher risk of drug and alcohol abuse).

Abortion has created the largest demographic in our American culture and throughout the world. The total number of deaths on US soil as a result of the September 11, 2001, terror-

---

[10] Unless otherwise noted, these statistics are provided by The Guttmacher Institute, Abort73, and the Centers for Disease Control.

[11] "Abortion for Profit," *Abort 73.com*, September 3, 2010, http://www.abort73.com/abortion/abortion_for_profit/.

ist attacks occur every single day (365 days a year) in abortion clinics throughout America. My heart cries out for those babies, parents, and families.

Many people believe that women can have an abortion and that it won't further affect anyone after the termination of the pregnancy. This is not true. You start with the baby, but the effects don't stop there. Many believe that between seven to nine people are profoundly affected by each abortion.[12] The abortion affects the mother both emotionally and physically. Abortion is an unnatural process that interrupts one of the primary functions of the human body. A woman's body naturally resists termination of a pregnancy, causing physical and emotional problems.

One of the most disturbing things about this procedure is that so many women are never informed about the consequences of an abortion. In 1986, the Supreme Court ruled that women don't have to be informed about these risks before the abortion. In later studies and surveys of women who experienced post-abortion symptoms, over 90 percent said "they were not given enough information to make an informed decision" and 83 percent said "it was very likely that they would have chosen differently if they had not been so strongly encouraged to abort by others, including their abortion counselor."[13]

Planned Parenthood's *Plan Your Children* pamphlet[14] stated, "An abortion kills the life of a baby after it has begun. It is dangerous to your life and health." That was in 1963. What happened in the span of ten years when *Roe v. Wade* was passed in

---

[12] "Into My Arms," (Worcester, PA: Vision Video, 2013), DVD.

[13] David Reardon, *Aborted Women: Silent No More* (Springfield, IL: Elliot Institute, 2002), 15-19.

[14] Planned Parenthood, *Plan Your Children,* (New York: n.p., 1963), 2.

1973? Did abortion suddenly become safe?

The legalization of abortion doesn't just affect the women who have abortions and the babies aborted. Abortion affects society as a whole. It devalues life. In the late 1960s and early 1970s, abortion rights supporters promised that through the legalization of abortion, society would be improved. Fewer teenagers would become pregnant. Child abuse would drop. Children would only live in homes that could support them. Children would live in more loving homes, and crime rates would drop. Yet, either because of or coincidentally with the ruling of *Roe v. Wade*, history has shown the opposite. Abortion has opened up an excuse to have uncontrolled behavior. Our society, and the children who have grown up in an abortion-filled world, have been negatively affected.

The impact abortion has on society is devastating. Although abortion proponents say that they want it to be safe and rare, it is now the most common medical procedure performed in the United States. It affects one in four pregnancies, and almost 40 percent of women who have had an abortion have had more than one. With over 1.2 million abortions performed each year in this country alone, you do the math. Even if you're not a mathematical wizard, it adds up to a whole lot of people.

If you were born after 1973, you're known as the "Survivor Generation," those who could have been aborted because of federal legalization of the procedure. Psychologists have now discovered "abortion survivor syndrome," a cluster of symptoms that mimic those of the soldiers who return from battle, and instead of feeling happy that they survived, they feel guilty and anxious. "Why wasn't I aborted instead of my sibling?"

We absolutely need better research surrounding the impact of abortion on individuals and society. That's difficult to accomplish due to the "shame and silence" that surrounds the subject of abortion. Some now theorize there is a causative link between abortion and child violence against other children in schools. By this devaluation of lives, making them disposable, some believe that children will not stop killing children until parents stop killing children.

Abortion weakens, and, quite often, destroys marriages and male-female relations in general. The woman who has aborted a child finds it more difficult to trust men. By lowering a woman's self-esteem, she becomes vulnerable to abusive relationships.

Some theorize that the very future of the church is dramatically affected by the abortion controversy. As the cancer of abortion becomes more embedded into the laws and framework of society, the more strained are the church's relations with government. The church must rely on the interaction with government leaders on a variety of programs that serve the people and advance the church's interests.

With attempts to limit public commentary on positions on abortion, there remains a cloaking effect on the freedom of the clergy to comment. This strains the authority of the church while an entire culture sits and waits to hear from those speaking from opposite positions.

Legal abortion distorts the purpose and slows medical progress. If defects in a child are handled by abortion, motivation to make medical progress in treating such defects is deterred. Equally, when embryos are destroyed, they can also be manipulated, experimented upon, sold, or combined with other species. There are huge implications of bioethical struggles in the future as a direct result.

Destroying over 57 million lives in a generation creates consequences— among them, fewer younger workers to support the system as an aging population retires from the workforce. Mother Teresa reportedly once said, "If we say that a mother can kill her own child, how can we tell other people not to kill each other? . . .The fruit of abortion is nuclear war."[15]

The post abortive are often known as "silent sufferers"—family members, neighbors, coworkers, those sitting next to us in church. With 43 percent of American women having had an abortion, there is a strong likelihood that half of the people you come in contact with have been affected by their decision to abort, many exhibiting symptoms of post-abortion stress.

A major part of healing a loss includes the grieving process. Grieving is a normal and healthy response to a major loss through death. It's a painful process, but one that helps to relieve sorrow. After an abortion, however, women often attempt to bury their grief, turn their emotions off, and run from God. Eventually, most face the fact that abortion ended their preborn baby's life.

Post-abortion grief results in getting "stuck" in unhealthy phases of grief, caused by the silence, shame, and guilt of having an abortion. There is no dead child to hold; no photographs; no funeral, burial, or grave to visit; no clergy. The only memories are of a rushed, painful procedure. After the abortion, reminders persist: the baby's expected delivery date, children of the same age, sounds at a dentist's office, a baby in a TV ad. It's only been in the last decade that many mental health professionals have started to recognize the many faces of post-abortion trauma.

Abortion choices create a situation of disenfranchised grief in women's lives. Disenfranchised grief is grief experienced by an individual that is not openly acknowledged, socially validated, or publically observed. The loss experienced is real, but survivors are not accorded the "right to grieve" by anyone around

[15]Mother Teresa (August 26, 1910–September 5, 1997) was a Roman Catholic religious sister and missionary who lived most of her life in Calcutta, India. She was the recipient of numerous honors, including the 1979 Nobel Peace Prize.

them.

A common effect of disenfranchised grief is depression, which manifests itself in small periods of sadness or more full-blown stints of depression. These periods may be accompanied by crying spells and low times, or "blue" days. Unprocessed grief can also cause people to "stay stuck" in anger without even realizing the source of their anger. Not connecting the depression with the unprocessed grief surrounding an abortion choice is typical.

Other ways to avoid "the abortion box" are medicating the pain with drugs or alcohol, becoming dependent on other people, and over medicating with food, which often leads to a full-blown eating disorder.

It is this tension of emotions—relief and sadness—that disrupts a woman's overall life and well-being. Unless she finds a safe place to talk and cry, she will probably live her life with a mask on, keeping her secret neatly tucked away out of fear, condemnation, or invalidation.

The counseling community has a saying: "Secrets kill." This is the path many women follow after abortion. Don't talk . . . don't feel . . . keep the secret . . . get on with life . . . even if it leads to death.

CHAPTER 10
A Ministry Is Born

*But I do not consider my life of any account as dear to
myself, so that I may finish my course and the ministry
which I received from the Lord Jesus, to testify solemnly
of the gospel of the grace of God.*

–ACTS 20:24

I made several trips to Austin between July 1 and July 9,
2013. Each trip proved to be as gut-wrenching as the last. By
the time I arrived home after my last trip on July 9, 2013, I felt I
had a pretty clear direction whether to start or not start a ministry. But after so many years of trial and error, I had learned it's
better to wait, then wait some more, before jumping from the
frying pan into the fire when making an important decision. I
wanted confirmation . . . I needed confirmation. Bent knees,
prayer, and wise counsel were instrumental in the final decision
process. By the end of 2013, though, the answer came—**GO
TELL IT!**

We prayed, we responded, we stepped out in faith, and with
the help of my friend and co-founder Karen, the collective ministries of Initiative 180 and its program of recovery, Peace After
the Storm, were born.

The announcement stated: "Today there is a mission field in

our churches and communities that has been created by abortion. Millions sit silently carrying the pain and heartache of shame and guilt, suffering severe life consequences. The collective ministries of Initiative 180, and its program of recovery, Peace After the Storm, have been created to serve as a healing resource and lifeline to anyone who has been wounded by abortion."

We seek confirmation about being in ministry continuously. Each time I'm ready to throw in the towel, complaining that ministry is just too hard, I receive some sign to continue . . . approval of our IRS 501(c)3 application within four months versus the normal eighteen-month waiting period, unexpected donations, volunteers who are excited about what we are doing, experts in marketing and graphic design, and encouragement from every corner.

Confirmations continue to come to us, although they may not look like a confirmation at the time. For several years my husband and I had been planning my retirement at the end of 2014, diligently working toward "our time." However, in May of 2014, I found out I had breast cancer. To the best of my knowledge, I have no family history of breast cancer, so to receive this news caught me by complete surprise, to say the least. My first thought was, "Ahem, Lord, what? I'm getting ready to retire and do real ministry stuff for You! This cancer diagnosis isn't in MY plans."

I was numb . . . actually scared speechless, if you want to know the truth. I tried to make sense of it all and started thinking: Was I feeling regret or fear? What was the difference? Well, regret is commonly regarded as remorse over the past; fear is typically anxiety for the future. If that's true, I now had both—regret and fear.

A cancer diagnosis tends to make the main thing the main thing. You're faced with fear of the unknown, reminders of your own mortality, and unresolved regrets from the past. Even though I'm no longer plagued with the guilt of a past choice (abortion), I still regret having made that decision. That single choice affected so many. Additionally, I've had regrets over words spoken in haste as well as words not spoken at all, remembering what I wished I had said at a friend's funeral.

Regret and fear can beat you up, for sure. So I was faced with this quandary as I processed through the cancer diagnosis. I was on my pity pot while I read (a lot). I calmed down by keeping my medical diagnosis in perspective. Plus, I decided not to focus so much on me (which was a real change, considering so much of my life was self-centered). But this I know: it was the prayers and encouragement of so many that kept me sane during the majority of 2014. Facing a lot of unknowns, I found comfort in the book of Psalms, which provided some much-needed salve to calm my deepest fears:

The LORD is my light and my salvation; Whom shall I fear?
The LORD is the defense of my life; Whom shall I dread?
−PSALM 27:1

Though a host encamp against me,
My heart will not fear; Though war arise against me,
In spite of this I shall be confident.
−PSALM 27:3

In 2014 I've had three cancer and reconstruction surgeries, and I'm happy to report (jubilant, to be exact) that I have a great prognosis (Stage I, zero nodes, no chemo or radiation necessary). The fear of cancer has not deterred me from my mission. I am pressing on!

"I was driving home late that night after work while listening to my favorite radio station. It was an evening talk show on the local Christian station. I heard a female voice talking about the same pain and emptiness I felt. Her story was taking me back and making me relive mine. Then she spoke about the peace she had found . . . I had to know more."[16]

—KAREN K. BRENNAND

---

[16] Karen K. Brennand, co-founder, Initiative 180 and its program of abortion recovery, Peace After the Storm.

CHAPTER 11
Transformation and Hope

And they overcame him because of the blood of the Lamb
and because of the word of their testimony, and they did not
love their life even when faced with death.
–REVELATION 12:11

KAREN

Karen was the first to respond to my testimony on the radio
program in January 2013. Hearing my story struck a chord in her.
She and I are co-founders of the collective ministries of Initiative
180 and Peace After the Storm.

* * *

I thought I had finally arrived. I no longer looked for a man's approval to try and make me feel complete. It had been thirteen years since my last divorce (actually this one was an annulment), and I was not sleeping around with any man who happened to smile at me, thinking it might be love. I was working at the same job for more than three years, living in a nice house, and paying my bills on time. Life was good . . . at least to where I thought was the level of happiness God would allow for me to experience because of the terrible action I had taken many years earlier.

In 1981, I was twenty-nine years old, divorced, in love, and pregnant. But my boyfriend, later to become my husband, did not want more children. Fear, abandonment, lack of support from my family or boyfriend, and denial that a real baby was living inside of me all contributed to my decision to have an abortion. Even my mother, who had chosen abortion in her past, suggested it would be the best thing for me. It was the easy solution, right? It was the quick fix to getting back to a normal life. Little did I know that decision to abort my baby would result in my life becoming an empty and isolated journey for the next thirty-two years, preventing me from developing any type of healthy self-worth or future meaningful relationships, personally or professionally.

My marriage to the father of my aborted baby quickly dissolved, and I became the "woman at the well" —running toward two additional marriages and even career after career—trying to find resolution and solace from the world instead of seeking God's grace, mercy, and forgiveness. I did everything to be perfect to make up for the bad I had done—marrying men who did not love me, working long overtime hours without monetary compensation or career recognition, and volunteering for any and all projects at church. It did not matter that I was physically and emotionally destroying myself, spiraling down further and further into depression, lack of self-worth, and anxiety—I found myself living with the inability to live. It was all I could do to just breathe. All the wrong choices I had continually made were my constant reminder that I would remain out of God's grace, and He would never recognize me again for any prayers of mercy or forgiveness. I knew this was my punishment, and I was not worthy of any future happiness.

Although I kept searching for peace with Bible study, church ministry, and participation in various healing study groups, the darkness continued to hold onto me. I knew God had decided to punish me. I would live the rest of this life single and childless. Yes, He loved me and I was saved, but He would keep me at arm's length. I had murdered my baby. I made the choices. I was guilty . . .

Now, as I continued listening to the radio program, I realized how my life had changed forever in 1981 because of my abortion. From the radio speakers, the woman's voice surrounded me in the car on that dark chilly night in January 2013, as if she was putting her arms around me, telling me she understood how I felt because she too had made that same decision many years ago. She knew my pain. She knew what it was like to live with the guilt and shame. She knew it all. She said we had a name. We were post-abortive. What? You mean other women have walked painful, destructive life journeys because of their abortion decisions? I thought I was just a bad person who would never have a normal, healthy lifestyle.

The radio program ended way too quickly. I wanted to know more. I wanted her peace. I wanted to have the relationship with Jesus that she said was available to me. I rushed home to my computer and the website she had mentioned on the air. I sent an email requesting information.

The nine-week post-abortive healing program began a few weeks later, and I went with trepidation. I was under the influence of Satan's lies that my life was as good as it was going to get. Did I really need any healing? I had dealt with all the past long ago. Why bring up old wounds again? Nevertheless, I walked into the group meeting as a hopeless Christian, knowing I was saved but certain I was forever lost because of what I had done.

With the caring love and commitment of these sisters in Christ who had also experienced an abortion in their past, I was able to trust their sensitive spirits and share my anger, hurt, and honest thoughts without any fear of misunderstanding or judgment. The program helped me to see God's unfailing forgiveness because of Christ's death and resurrection—no matter what my past involved. These women helped me to realize that nothing could separate me from His COMPLETE and FULL love . . . NOTHING.

Through this post-abortion healing program, my life was changed again forever! After thirty-two years, there is now a joyful ending (or should I say, a new beginning) to my story. My sin had made me a slave to painful shame and guilt, but now I am free with the peace of Jesus that surpasses any understanding. This life here on earth will never give me the sweet sounds of my child's laughter or memories of him running into my arms for a precious hug. But I know that my son is with Jesus for all eternity and that I will see him someday when I am called home. He and I will hug each other and recognize our love as only a mother and child can. God has given even me the priceless gift of forgiveness.

Mother's Day was the grand finale for me in that year of transformation in 2013. For the first time, I was able to stand up in church to be recognized as a mother. I AM A MOTHER. What an amazing feeling that gives me every time I say those words. That day was the most joyous and beautiful experience of my life. God's grace is life changing!

If I had known in 1981 what I know now about the lifelong, self-destructive behaviors associated with those who have had an abortion, I would have NEVER taken that first step into the abortion clinic. I would have sought wise counsel from those who know more on the subject, listened to my baby's heartbeat, or viewed his sonogram. The consequences of my decision will never go away, but God remembers our past no more. HE has given us new life through Christ Jesus, HIS only Son, who died and conquered death to rise again so that we can live free and forgiven from the choices that have kept us in bondage for so many years. God walked with me every painful step of the way after my decision to have an abortion, and he also waited for me to finally turn around and receive His full gift of forgiveness.

No matter what wrong paths you may have chosen in your life journey, know that YOU are the beloved child of Holy God. I can assure you that He loves you and is *always* with you. His word is living testimony that will fill you with His grace and mercy through the love of Christ. Just seek Him and you will find Him. All you have to do is knock, and the door of forgiveness will be opened to you. He will not let go of you. Turn around. He is holding His arms wide open for you, too!

VICKI

Earlier in my story I referred to a friend from my old neighborhood who was instrumental in my seeking an abortion-recovery Bible study. Neither of us knew then what the result would be of my attending that abortion-recovery retreat. See what happens when a story is shared in a simple conversation?

* * *

In 1994 I was talking to a customer at Mama's Daughters' Diner, a restaurant that I owned with my family in the West End area of Dallas. His name was Harry, and he was the Sunday school director at First Baptist Church of Dallas. He asked me, "Do you have a church home?" I replied, "I don't, but am looking for one (which I was!)."

He invited me to attend First Baptist, which I did with my sister-in-law. One Sunday, after a few times visiting the church, I heard the new director of the Downtown Pregnancy Center talk about the ministry there. I had never heard about such a ministry before that helped women with unplanned pregnancies. I didn't think much more about it, because honestly, I didn't want to. But that didn't stop me from joining the church that year in 1994.

Fast-forward to 2005: I was sitting in my Sunday school class one Sunday morning and a fellow member asked the class if someone could help her in the Wee Care Shoppe of the Downtown Pregnancy Center. A couple of weeks went by, and I checked with her to see if she had found anyone to help. She had not. Feeling bad that no one had offered, I said that I would be willing to help with sorting baby clothes and other non-interactive tasks.

Well, the next week after I began, volunteer training for counselors at the Downtown Pregnancy Center was being offered, and I thought to myself that I could probably talk to girls about an unplanned pregnancy because I had been in that circumstance many years ago.

So I signed up for the intensive training. I learned so much about abortion. I had hoped that I would never have to think about my own abortion back in 1971. But, here I was thinking . . . what?! . . . *why*?!!

Note the date of my abortion so long ago. Yes, it was before the passing of *Roe v. Wade*, which legalized abortion. My own was an illegal abortion, a referral by our trusted family doctor. This was a dark part of my past which I worked hard to forget.

Well, the "why" was that God had a plan and purpose for my life. He wanted me to go through post-abortion healing. He wanted me to experience complete forgiveness from the guilt and shame that I had felt for over thirty-five years, and He evidently wanted me to serve Him through ministry with the Downtown Pregnancy Center, now a part of Involved for Life, Inc. (IFLI).

I was called to move from volunteering to join the staff in 2006 and have watched God grow this ministry considerably in the years since I have been serving at IFLI. The number of babies saved from abortion has grown from twenty-seven to over four hundred per year, the number of women who have trusted Christ as their Savior has continued to grow as well, and the Uptown Women's Center and Sonograms on Site ministry arms were added.

I know that my "story" would have ended differently had there been a pregnancy center to go to back in 1971. I know that I would have chosen life for my baby had I seen a sonogram, heard a heartbeat, and had more facts.

I believe that God called me to this ministry because He knew that I would know, firsthand, the extreme value of the free services that we provide. He created a desire in me to arm women and girls with facts to make an informed choice regarding their unplanned pregnancy. I want others to have what I missed out on: a chance to make a choice without regret.

There are over 2,800 names in our ministry's donor database—they represent the people who have partnered with us in one way or another over the years. I can only imagine the countless stories represented in the "why" they became involved. Most likely, their stories are similar to mine. That is how Debby and I became friends, as I got to know her as one of our ministry supporters. As she shared her past with me, I was able to share with her the positive impact that comes from post-abortion healing.

My greatest joy comes in helping others make a better choice when they find themselves with an unplanned pregnancy and from sharing the hope and healing that is possible for those who have been a part of abortion. Like so many others who were Christians when they had their abortion, I knew in my head I was forgiven, but to truly experience that forgiveness in my heart through a post-abortion healing weekend was a transformational experience. I look forward to the day when I hold my daughter, Sunny, in my arms when we're reunited in heaven!

KIM

Kim was my first co-facilitator for the initial abortion recovery group at Involved for Life. Kim's story is a testament to the power of what a surrendered life can do for others. She's an awesome woman of God.

* * *

We all have a story. I'd heard that line, but I didn't understand it until I started actually sharing mine. I think now everyone's stories are just shades of different colors. Some, more red; some, more blue; some, more yellow—and some are just more *juicy*.

When I was five years old, I used to run in the door from my half-day kindergarten to watch *I Love Lucy*. My Mom and I referred to her as "juicy Lucy." And I just loooved Lucy! I got her; I understood her. She talked too much, was always seeking adventure, and was forever getting into trouble. She always stuck out, and even though she drove everyone crazy, they all deep down loved her and loved being around her. I've spent years trying to tone down my "Lucy" until I was able to stand back and see that Lucy is ME. And the me that I was created to be is OK.

You see, I was adopted at three months old from an unwed mother's home. Raised in a wonderful home in the most perfect town, I was given everything and more. As an adopted child, I always had an "I wonder" in my heart. I didn't know anything about my birth family when I was young, and maybe I just felt a connection to Lucy's character as a young five-year-old already trying to figure out who she was. Unlike the TV character, my adventurous side turned from cute and boisterous to risky.

I was not only the loudest but also the drunkest and most devious, creating master plans to party and play while maintaining a mostly "good girl" image. While I was an "A" student, athlete, and friend, I was also constantly in search of love through guys whom I dated, slept with, and had one night stands with, some even in my teen years. Between alcohol and a reputation, I slowly opened the door to a truly wicked heart. Even those things that happened in my life that were considered unfair—dark things that I didn't ask for or deserve—happened because I was totally enslaved to my desire for love.

It's interesting now to understand that I was emotionally, spiritually, and physically addicted to love. There's an actual chemical reaction inside you through the entire process of meeting, flirting with, kissing, and ultimately, having sex with another person. As I crashed from this high, I would be back out looking for it again and again. Of course, I tried desperately to be better, even if it was fleeting. And there were good times . . . I had lots of friends, great memories, even a handful of accomplishments. There were some sweet boys whom I dated and attended dances with.

As I entered college I hoped for a clean slate—a chance to start anew and be better. If only life were as easy as a thirty-minute sitcom that starts fresh with each episode. Despite an imperfect beginning in the college world, I did meet a smart, funny guy and quickly fell in love. It was special and crazy and intense. The freedom you have in college to love someone almost 24/7 is easy to fall into. We were pretty inseparable, and after a few months of the relationship, I found myself pregnant.

Gosh, what would Lucy do now? In a TV sitcom, you barely even see what the outcome of a circumstance is twenty-four hours later! It wasn't long after watching the stick change to a plus sign in that last stall of the bathroom shared by the entire floor of a dormitory that I knew what I had to do.

Wasn't it obvious? Wasn't it an unspoken rule? College girls don't get pregnant—or, at least, they don't stay that way. I had never seen one—not on my campus or any of my friends'. I did what I thought everyone did. I went to the clinic, and within minutes they confirmed I was pregnant. After a few more minutes, I was handed the number to an abortion clinic and told that I would be all right. There was no mention of a baby, an option, or any kind of support, never mind a warning about the potential risks of the choice I was making.

And so, I called that number. I remember wishing someone would stop me—but who would? My friends were just relieved that it wasn't them. The minute I woke up from the procedure that day, I remember crying uncontrollably, because even though all I heard before that day was, "You'll be all right," the minute it was over, all I could hear was, "How could you?" The shame and immediate realization of what I did that poured over me was unbearable. And so I buried it down deep as far as I could and went on with my life.

And I survived, mostly. After years of further struggle of good, bad, better, and worse, I did mature and graduate college. I also landed a great job and got married. Then, before I was married, I had to return to church: I mean if you want to get married in one, you have to start attending again! This time it was a different kind of church—and I was tired of holding it all together. It was there that I had to face my past and fully understand that I could never fix it, change it, or make up for it. I handed it over and finally surrendered everything to the God of the universe who loved me—even during my darkest, saddest, most painful days.

When I accepted Jesus and was baptized, I took the biggest brush and painted all my sin and all my past a new color: WHITE. Unbelievable!! And God poured into me throughout the days that followed through church, study, friends, and neighbors. But I was still so broken and messy; I had major cracks in this new foundation that was being formed. Instead of learning about God, I learned how to look Christian. And although the learning was never wasted, those cracks were shaking the whole foundation.

That world came crashing down in my early thirties. It was ugly. After three children, two states, and four houses, I was depressed, lonely, and lost. Turning my back on God, I visited some of my old habits. How did I return to this place? I'm miles and years away from my "juicy Lucy" days. Or am I? Have I ever really changed? It was time for me to stop looking Christian and figure out how to have the faith I'd seen and heard about from so many people around me. With Christ by my side and many friends' prayers, I found the way . . .

And God continued to push me toward complete surrender. You see, He had started to place a call on my life—one I could never imagine.

At the same time that I was realizing my need for a truly authentic faith, I attended a luncheon for a pregnancy center. At the time I didn't even know exactly what a pregnancy center was. You see, a friend had a "hunch" that I might have had an abortion in my past. The speaker on stage that afternoon paused in the middle of what she was sharing and said, "If anyone here has experienced abortion and never spoken to anyone about it, you need to, even if it was fifteen years ago." That woman, just like the author of this book, has spent years standing in the gap for women like me. She shares that same fire, passion, grace, and tenderness for women who've experienced abortion. She took God's spotlight that day and shined it directly at me so that I could not escape. You see, my abortion was almost exactly fifteen years to the day.

She knew what Debby knows—that there were women there that day who were suffering in silence. Statistics don't lie. She knew there would be at least one post-abortive Christian woman who was dragging heavy ankle weights around as she walked into church and Bible study, poured herself into her family, and tucked her pain away where grace wasn't allowed. That day, it was me. I had spent years continuing to understand and celebrate that I had been forgiven, but I also travelled through life heavy and punished. I shared my hidden truth with my friend that day. A week later, I connected with that pregnancy center and started down a new path.

As I entered this pro-life world, I began sharing my story even before I had completed the required post-abortion healing. It's funny to me now: God allowed my story to be used on video and even shared at my church in front of thousands before I even understood the power of His healing. I think He allowed me to speak out because I was being obedient to His call and others' needs. I felt undeserving to be sharing my abortion with others, but I had a very clear grasp of all that God had done for me and that my story was really one of redemption.

You see, if God can use a mess like me, He can use anyone. That day, the day I said yes to sharing my story, it put me exactly on the path that God wanted me on. I said yes to the one thing—the first thing. Ironically, the first time my story was filmed, the lighting was insufficient, and the film couldn't even be used. But that day, there was a woman who stood behind the camera. It was the first time I ever spoke about the pain of my abortion out loud. I remember watching tears roll down her face—and I was shocked that my story touched someone so deeply. It was the beginning of my realization that my story had power—for others and me. She was the first person who acknowledged the pain I had felt, and it served as yet another step toward removing those heavy ankle weights.

I finally attended a retreat for women who experienced abortion and felt fully surrendered to God's love as a result. That only came from sitting across from Christ, without anything between us, and putting my broken heart into His lap. He held it while I grieved and mourned and finally asked for repentance over the lifestyle that had led to that decision years ago as a college student. God's grace IS sufficient. I had to admit just how lost I was, with NO excuses. I also had to understand that I had offended my God and Father and admit that it resulted in my choosing to end the life of my daughter.

Now, there's an endless overflowing of grace, love, and healing. That process introduced me to what complete surrender is and how it is necessary to truly feel and accept complete healing from God. And there is NO substitute. I could not be the person I am today without it. Grace isn't just the trickle that I had been depending on for so long. It's a faucet turned on all the way, filled with His love and His mercy that can permeate the darkest crevices of our soul.

As I have progressed in my healed newness, I have met some of the most incredibly passionate and strong women. The author of this book shines the spotlight on others in need and calls them to the very special surrender and healing necessary when you've experienced abortion. Through her I have come to confirm that only God can take your talent, your story, and your passion and use it to impact His people.

It's amazing to watch that happen in someone else's life. I remember the first time I experienced it. This woman was in my boss's office talking about a post-abortion study and her effort to reach out to women who were hurting. I was like that little girl in front of the TV screen watching Lucille Ball. I got her. I agreed with her, and I loved the fire that burned within her for helping women find freedom in Christ through this unique process.

Debby has also taught me the power of sharing your story. I used to think that it was a step you could skip, or maybe it was for some women, but not others. Since then, I've come to realize that sharing your story doesn't mean that you need to write a book or post your story for the world to see. It can be as simple as sharing it with your best friend.

I recently saw the change on a young woman's face as she told me she had done this, shared her story for the first time with a friend. I remember she acknowledged it by saying, "I realize it's OK now, and it's just part of my life." She looked lighter; she looked free. And I believe that this step helped her in a way neither she nor I expected!

You see, it helped her become more of the Lucy she was meant to be—free to love, free to laugh, and free to enjoy life without the burden of a decision she made years before. To paraphrase David in Psalm 103, the Lord can renew your youth through His love and mercy. That's why we all loved Lucy—she is young at heart! And now women like me—and others I've seen transformed through His healing—can be too.

I am grateful for those women who are committed to removing that burden from women and men just like me.

Bless the LORD, O my soul, and all that is within me, bless his holy name! Bless the LORD, O my soul, and forget not all his benefits, who forgives all your iniquity, who heals all your diseases, who redeems your life from the pit, who crowns you with steadfast love and mercy, who satisfies you with good so that your youth is renewed like the eagle's. (Pss. 103:1-5)

JULIA

Julia is a friend and fellow church member. She heard my testimony for the first time at the concert. After several months, she confided to me that she, too, had had an abortion.

* * *

Can you keep a secret? I can. For thirty-five years, I kept my teenaged abortion a secret. No one was ever supposed to know. Not my parents, not my extended family, not my children—*no* one would ever know because I would carry this secret with me to my grave.

I certainly didn't want the people in my church to know, the people I sat in pews with and sang in choirs with and whose children I cared for in nurseries. How would they ever understand the terrible thing I had done? I was convinced that they wouldn't, because I was certain that nothing as ugly as abortion had ever crossed their perfect paths.

Only, I was wrong. Someone who looked like me, lived like me, and worshiped like me stood up at the front of my church one Sunday morning and testified about the truth of her abortion, her secrets, and the tangled web of lies she spun around herself. She spoke about the burden of keeping a really big secret that she was really ashamed of, one she regretted with all her heart. She spoke about the same secrets I carefully hid under my smooth, I've-got-it-all-together façade.

I remember she said, through her calm tears, that she had never even given her baby a chance. And that's when something I thought I had long ago buried began to resurrect in me. It was through watching her peaceful countenance—*while confessing an ugly truth about herself*—and listening to her speak about healing and forgiveness that I began to understand that even the sin of abortion can come into the light of day through genuine confession and repentance—and that Christ could forgive me and begin to heal the shame I had lived with for so long.

I knew I wanted her peace, and I believed for the first time in my life that it was even possible. I wanted to be free from the self-inflicted punishment and panic that I lived with any time the topic of abortion came up in conversation. If it was really possible to dig up my hidden secret and offer it once and forever to Jesus to completely forgive; if I could then live in such a way that abortion no longer occupied that deepest, guiltiest spot in my heart—then I was interested. She definitely had my attention!

And so, I began a post-abortion Bible study at my church, walking on a path that others had trod to find light and truth and healing. It wasn't easy and it wasn't a quick fix. It was a trail of tears that went deeper and deeper into dark places before I reached the clearing and the view opened up to the promise I had hoped for. It was led by post-abortive women who understood firsthand about the awful truth we have ingested because we swallowed the lies dished up by an abortion-peddling culture—and spoon-fed to us by our own selfish selves.

Through the Bible study, I found the courage to ask my own baby for forgiveness. I was able to dignify his short life by giving him a name and grieving his memory in a way I had never allowed myself the freedom to experience before. It was hard, but it was ever so healing. I went through the lessons with the other women, and we helped each other and held each other. We were members in the largest women's club that nobody wants to admit belonging to.

One day I will hold my precious baby in my arms, and we will have those tender times together that should have been ours those many years ago. The tears that we will shed as we embrace for the first time will be free from regret and shame and recrimination. They will spill over us with a cleansing flow, sweet and refreshing from Christ's well of living water.

I am grateful my church offers this class in which members and non-members participate. I'm really thankful for the testimony that shattered my secret world that Sunday and set me on a path to honesty and healing. I am certain that there are many others, sitting in pews and office cubicles and at kitchen tables, silent and broken and suffering, who will never be whole until they surrender their own secret.

Now I participate in boldly speaking out against abortion and in speaking *in support* of those women who have been hurt by past abortions. In fact, I would say that my life is now dedicated to that endeavor. I have gone from expecting to die with my secret to opening up and letting go of it in the most public way that I never dreamed of. Now I expect to really live in openness and honesty, forgiven and set free.

ISLEE

Islee heard my testimony on the radio and responded. She waited until God told her it was time to go through the Bible study. What a change we saw in her! She's a blessing to everyone and has blossomed into a beautiful Godly woman.

* * *

I was a nineteen-year-old single mom in my first year of college when I learned I was pregnant. Unfortunately, I still remember it like it was yesterday. The father of the baby and I were freaked out that the baby may have some illness because our child was conceived on the typical overindulgent prom night. The crisis pregnancy clinic told us that the fetus was actually a baby. They showed us videos of women who regretted their abortion and how the procedure would take place if I chose to abort. I remember feeling lost and hopeless, and no matter how the dad felt, I automatically felt ten times worse due to the fact that the baby was inside of ME. My close friend had multiple abortions and she seemed fine, mentally and physically. She encouraged me to get one. She said (along with many others) that the baby would ruin my career, friendships, and my life. I was supposed to be working with fashion designers and on my way to owning my own company.

I was supposed to be the one in my family to "make it" to help everyone out. The reality of my life was caving in on me. Even though the father of the baby loved me and wanted to start a life with me, I just couldn't. No matter how hard I tried to choose life, it seemed as if death surrounded me. I chose abortion. I chose to give up the life growing within me in exchange for heartache and regret. The unfortunate thing is that deep down, I knew that it was wrong, yet I did it anyway.

After my abortion, I felt lost. I felt as if I made one of the biggest mistakes in my life, and there was nothing I could do to turn back the clock. Even in a room filled with people, I felt so alone. I knew that I had made a choice that I would end up regretting for the rest of my life. That day I aborted my baby, something inside of me died too. My addiction to drugs and alcohol got worse. I was just trying to mask my pain. I was torn and in pieces.

I met Christ a short time after my abortion. I thought everything was OK, that I didn't have any emotional baggage that I was carrying around, but I was wrong. God really began to deal with me on the healing I needed inside of my mind and soul from the abortion. I heard a broadcast on the radio about a woman who was healed in her heart from her past abortion. This woman sounded so free to speak about her mistake and genuine in wanting to help others find the same freedom she had. I knew I had to call and sign up for the next Bible recovery class. I was afraid and saw myself as such a failure before the class. I had some hope, but I always feared the worse for my life and doubted God about His best for me. After the class, I realized that these feelings were tied to my abortion. I didn't know God forgave me once and for all for my sin. I learned that He not only forgave me but also that He wasn't angry with me . . . nor did He expect me to "pay Him back" for what I did.

I now live guilt- and shame-free. I can talk and testify about my experience freely. Although I regret my choice, I am able to move on with my life instead of having my feet stuck in the mud of the past. I am free, I am loved, and I am forgiven. God used the Bible study recovery class and the women who shared their lives with me to change my life, and I will never be the same. I am renewed.

DAWN

Dawn has been a volunteer at the pregnancy center for several years. She responded to a call for volunteers for a new post-abortion ministry at church. She leads recovery Bible studies and shares her story at every opportunity, giving hope to many.

* * *

I have lived through four pregnancies out of wedlock. I am not proud of what I did in the past, but I have been healed from the hurt of abortion and am using my past experiences to help others.

My first pregnancy occurred when I was in high school at the age of sixteen. I really did not know what to do or how I would tell my parents. I remember that day so well, talking to the two of them in the family room. They sat in their chairs, and I sat shaking inside. Somehow, the words came out. I don't remember much from the conversation except that I was a disgrace to the family. The family decision was to abort my first child.

My second pregnancy occurred when I was twenty-three years old. I was not living at home, but I was living a life involving alcohol, drugs, and sex, and I had not married yet. I do not remember telling my parents, but I do remember Mother taking me to a pregnancy center where I chose to give my son up for adoption.

My third pregnancy occurred when I was thirty-one and in college. I was looking for love in all the wrong places. I thought my life was really going pretty well: I had kicked the bad drug habit, and I was finally going to get a bachelor's degree. There just was no time to have a baby, so I chose to abort my third child.

My fourth pregnancy occurred when I was thirty-three years old. I had a great job and had dated a couple guys since I moved to Dallas. The second person I dated really made me feel special, and one thing led to another, and then I was pregnant. Unfortunately, I knew where he stood: e he had already told me that if I ever got pregnant, he would want me to get an abortion because he did not want to lose face with his family. I chose to deliver my son and cut the man out of my life.

My life changed dramatically after my fourth child was born. I learned so much, but one of the biggest discoveries was unconditional love. The unconditional love came from the fact that my son Garrison loved me and that I loved him, even though he did nothing but eat and sleep.

While raising Garrison, twenty-seven years after my first pregnancy, something hit me like a brick. I missed my daughter, whom my parents decided to have aborted. I knew she was a girl because during my abortion, I heard the doctor say it was a girl. I was so far along in my pregnancy that they could tell the sex. I sought help, and during this time, I named my child Susan Paula. Susan, because I had never known a Susan I did not like, and Paula after her father, Paul. I went through weeks of mourning, missing the life of my little Susan.

While healing from the pain of missing Susan, I almost had a nervous breakdown because I had put my third child's abortion so far back in my mind that I did not believe I made the decision myself to terminate my pregnancy. No one in my family knew I had this abortion, and when my thoughts surrounding this abortion returned, I fell on my knees and was literally sobbing with tears. I finally picked up the phone and told my mother what I had done. I named this child Michael.

A year after that, I wanted to find my second child I had given up for adoption. I started with the agency I gave him up through, and after two calls, they said they found him. To this day, I have not met him, but I have had the opportunity to speak to—and become Facebook friends with—his mother. A healing moment for me was when I heard, "Thank you so much for the gift you have given our family." I named him Stanley Jesse at birth, but his family renamed him. He now has a little girl who looks like me when I was little. One day we may meet, but for now, Stanley has decided not to meet me. This does not weaken his mother's and my relationship, however.

I want you to know that I truly regret the fact that two of my children died by the means of abortion. When I had my two abortions, I did not know it was wrong in the eyes of God. My mother took me to church every chance she got, but my father never went with us. I became a Christian after my fourth son, Garrison, was little. My babysitter for Thursday-night bowling invited me to church. I walked in the church in April, and by August I accepted Jesus as my Lord and Savior. This started a new life for me. I quit smoking and drinking. I attended church on a regular basis.

When Garrison was in kindergarten, I put him in a Christian school downtown, close to where I worked. It was a Christian school connected to a very large church with a rich heritage. We lived way north of town in the suburbs, and when I decided to move closer to work, I also decided to change churches. Out of the mouth of my baby, Garrison said, "Why don't you go to church where I go to school?" I thought the church was too big, but we visited and joined soon after. One of this church's ministries was a pregnancy center. I felt God was really pulling me in the direction to serve there. Who could better minister to someone in a crisis pregnancy than someone who had walked in their shoes? It took me months to send my paperwork in, but once I did, the director called me, and I made an appointment to meet with her.

One of the questions she asked me was if I had ever had an abortion. My heart filled up with shame, and I finally shared that I had, and I broke down in tears for the first time in twenty-seven years. She listened to my story and told me that in order to serve at the pregnancy center, I would have to go through a post-abortion Bible study. I accepted the challenge, and believe you me, that is what it was to show up every week for twelve weeks. I noticed my sadness began to diminish with each class. I then started serving and counseling women who were pregnant.

Due to my health, I had to take a break from serving at the pregnancy center for a few years. When I felt I was strong enough, it was time for me to return. Just about this time, there was a woman who had shared her testimony in church, and I met her through the pregnancy center. Her mission was to help those who had abortions through abortion-recovery Bible studies.

I am now serving my God in two entities of abortion: I am talking to abortion-minded women at the pregnancy center and facilitating post-abortion Bible study classes. Who would have thought that I would share my children, Susan and Michael? My children will always be alive in my heart, and their short lives are allowing me help other mothers choose life along with helping others heal from the hurt of abortion and explaining how much God loves them. I have seen God at work in women's lives when they become free of shame, guilt, and the terror of their past abortions. At the writing of this book, my living children are twenty-three and thirty-three years old. I know the day will come when I will be with all my children in heaven. In the meantime, I am happy; I lean on my Lord's strength to do what He wants me to do. I have discovered that when you obey, life is easier than when you live under the constant shadow of doubt.

AMANDA

Amanda was intentional in her search for abortion recovery. After several attempts, we made contact and she joined one of our recovery groups. I have seen her faith blossom each time she shares her story.

* * *

I was raised in the church but did not understand what a personal relationship with Christ meant. I really remember learning about the dos and don'ts and the "rules" of the church, but I don't remember learning about grace. When I went off to college, I stopped going to church because that was where the "perfect" people were, and I certainly did not feel perfect.

My life took a dramatic turn the day I found out I was pregnant. Once again, this was something I was not going to let out. How could a girl from a Christian home ever be pregnant without being married? I always wanted to be the one who waited for marriage, so how could I face the world and let them see that I had messed up? So I buried my secret, put on a happy face, and chose abortion because I thought it would be a solution. Little did I know how much pain this choice would create. From day one, I was buried in guilt and shame; a part of me died that day along with my baby girl, Marilyn Joy. That day, two people's dreams were killed. I thought I could just push the pain away, just as I did with every other negative thing that had happened in my life. At this time, I was not active in church. I thought God was really upset with me, and I could not be forgiven for my mistakes, let alone my abortion.

Eventually, I did start going to church and started to understand the concept of grace. I prayed fervently for Jesus to help me. All this time, He was slowing showing me how to live His way. I was still struggling with the old habit of pretending.

In 2009 all my secrets came to a crashing halt. I had a nervous breakdown on Mother's Day weekend. My physicians told me I was suffering from bipolar disorder and schizophrenia. I began to talk about all the issues I had hidden: my abortion, my trouble with money, etc. I became totally honest with a few people for the first time in my life. I now know I was suffering from both the trauma of my abortion and the way I had always dealt with life—by sweeping things under the rug and being too afraid to talk about them. I would teeter back and forth on giving my burdens over to Him, then taking everything back. There was one thing, though, I wasn't ready to give up—one thing I thought couldn't be forgiven—my abortion. This "secret" was keeping me from getting well.

God kept working on my heart and led me to a recovery Bible study. That was one of the most eye-opening Bible studies I have ever participated in. I know today that all my mistakes are wiped clean because of what Christ did on the cross for ME. He knew the choices I would make, and that is why He chose to come to this earth to die for ME, because he loved me, a sinner, that much. I am assured that all things work together for the good of those who love God. I understand the power of forgiveness and realize that I have to forgive because I have been forgiven. I understand that God loves me perfectly and wants the best for me, and nothing can ever separate me from His love. I can now take all my experiences and go tell the world of Christ's love and really understand it. I hope to help people really understand the Gospel and know that it is for them. I am ready to be a light in this dark world and help expel the lies the enemy has brought to this world—because I am free in CHRIST, and I can do anything with Him by my side.

KRYSTAL

After many years, Krystal knew she needed help and sought an abortion-recovery Bible study to heal her broken heart. I'm glad she found our ministry.

* * *

My childhood was bright as the sunshine. I had a great home life along with my two siblings. I have always clung to Christ and was never interested in living the fast-paced lifestyle. My passion as a child and to this day was to pursue music.

It was my abortion in 1996 when I was seventeen that destroyed so much of my life. As a senior in high school, I fell to peer pressure. I wanted to be like everyone else. The result was being unmarried, single, and without support. I never thought I would end up sitting inside an abortion clinic discussing with doctors how I could terminate my pregnancy.

I made the decision alone and went to the clinic alone. The clinic told me I would be OK and that everything would be fine. I was told that I was making the right decision because I could still have children one day, just not today. I wanted to run away from the clinic, but I couldn't move.

After the abortion, I noticed I was afraid to trust or form relationships with others. I was never told I could suffer consequences after the abortion; no one ever mentioned the emotional trauma or that I would be angry at myself and everyone around me.

After many years, I wanted to surrender my secret of abortion, so I began to search online for a post-abortion ministry. While searching for help, I was feeling very hopeless. I was flooded with reminders of how I tried to reach as a seventeen-year-old girl and had not received any help.

After much prayer, I read online about Christ-centered Bible study designed for women like me. I responded through emails and telephone calls. I learned that the ministry was nine weeks long. After beginning the study, the hope and compassion expressed through the women involved with this ministry helped provide hope to me. Today I am able to bond, and my anger has diminished. I am at peace.

I was told at the abortion clinic that my abortion was not wrong. But Christ is using my negative experience for the positive to help prevent other young teenagers today from making the same mistake I made. There is hope and help after the storm of abortion. Christ has worked a miracle in me through this ministry.

CHARITY

Charity walked into our ministry as a referral from another ministry. Her charming smile is infectious and grows brighter every time we meet. God is doing a great work in our sweet Charity.

* * *

The female nurse asked me to remove all my clothes. She handed me an itchy gown and slippers in return. I felt humiliated, mortified, and ashamed. My stomach turned as I stood there. The nurse's instructions were drowned out by the moans and screams of the other patients. I felt weak. My head started to spin as I was led to a room full of reclining chairs. I was given a thin blanket, and I immediately covered my head. I began to cry softly. The woman next to me murmured under her breath, "Lord, Jesus, don't let them get me. They've taken my family. They've taken all I had. Jesus, they're coming for me. Help me, Jesus! Help me!" After two hours of this, I thought the same thing: "Jesus, help me. How did I get here?" In just another hour, I would be missing a highly anticipated acting workshop. I had paid hundreds of dollars and waited months to have an opportunity to perform in front of one of the foremost casting directors in the film industry. This was supposed to be my day to shine, my day to make a lasting impression, but instead I was sedated, in a psych ward, with dried blood on my wrists.

I didn't get there overnight. It wasn't a single isolated event or one bad choice. It was a series of poor decisions. One bad choice compounded by another led me to that psychiatric hospital in handcuffs. I do clearly remember, though, the catalyst for my self-destructive behavior: my abortion. I wholeheartedly believe that having my child would have been far easier than to suffer through than the heartache, pain, anger, numbness, and self-loathing that many post-abortive men and women experience.

At the time of my pregnancy, I was on a break from my boyfriend of roughly five years. I'll call him Jordan (not his real name). We had been living together in San Antonio without the knowledge of my parents. Unhappy with the circumstances of our relationship, I decided to move back home to my family in Dallas. I needed to reevaluate my life and choices. I still loved Jordan; I just didn't love his choices.

I immediately reconnected with friends in town. I wanted to have fun and be carefree. I began to drink heavily and party often. My heart was broken. I missed Jordan. Although we spoke occasionally, the chance for reconciliation seemed dismal, so I drank that much more. One night, after moving back home, I met Chris (not his real name). We had quite a few mutual friends. Chris and I had gone to high school together, but we had never associated with one another. He was the proverbial "bad boy." The first night we hung out, he was very quiet. He seemed nervous. I remember thinking he had such a great smile. Alcohol and partying was the common denominator that kept Chris and me together. Our friendship escalated quickly, and eight months later, I was pregnant.

My initial reaction was fear. My father had just gone to jail, leaving behind a large mortgage and a distressed wife. How would my family be able to cope with the added pressure of a newborn? I didn't have a degree, and I was making ends meet as a bartender at a seedy downtown bar. How could I afford this child? I barely knew Chris, and what I did know was not comforting. He was in and out of mental hospitals and rehab. He was a whirlwind of chaos, and I was caught in its wake. To make matters worse, I was still in love with Jordan, and he was desperately in love with me. He said he had been saving money ever since I left, sleeping on couches to eventually move to Dallas. He wanted to reconcile with me and eventually marry.

I was disgusted with myself. How could I be so reckless and irresponsible? How could I be so naive to think that unprotected sex wouldn't lead to a crisis pregnancy? I took three more tests hoping that there was a mistake. It all felt so surreal. I called Chris and told him I was pregnant. I told him to meet me in the park, where I gave him the positive pregnancy test. He was just as shocked as I was. Before I considered what I was saying, I blurted out, "I'm not keeping it." I'm not sure if those were even my words. It sounded like my voice, but it's almost as if someone was speaking for me. I was shocked at my resolve. There were several moments of silence. Finally, Chris said, "No. I can't support that. I want to keep the baby." I didn't know what was more alarming: being pregnant or Chris wanting to keep the baby. I was floored. I was so paralyzed by fear that I didn't consider there to be any other option. I told Chris that with or without him, I was going to have an abortion. So, reluctantly, he agreed to support me. Chris, like so many other men, believed the lie that he had no say in the pregnancy. "My body; my choice" is the most destructive lie we both believed that day. Chris' heart was breaking, but he had no way to articulate his feelings to me. I was being driven by fear, and nothing else mattered more than getting back to "normal."

At the same time, Jordan was moving back to Dallas in hopes of winning my heart. The timing could not have been worse. I called Jordan to tell him the truth. I told him "I'm pregnant. It's not yours, but I still love you." The only thing I hear was sobbing. "Hello?" I said into the receiver. More sobbing. I'd never heard anyone cry like that before. I felt like a monster. The moments that followed seemed to stretch into an eternity. When Jordan had finally composed himself, he said "I love you too. I love you so much. I can forgive you. I still want to be with you . . . I just can't raise another man's baby. I can't." I'm not sure what I expected him to say. I thought he would be repulsed and angry. I mean, I repulsed and angered myself. Sometimes I think it would have been easier if he would have just abandoned the idea of us altogether, but he didn't. He said, "It's your choice and your life, but I can't be with you and raise another man's child." The conversation ended abruptly, and I went home to think.

Depression began to set in. My thoughts grew more morbid with each passing day. "The longer you wait, the worse it'll be," I told myself. I researched abortion clinics online. I found one I thought would be suitable and asked Jordan to take me. The following day we arrived at a dilapidated building without a sign. It was repulsive and dirty. I wouldn't have left my dog unattended in these streets, much less come here to consult a doctor, but here I was. We walked into the building hand in hand. I looked around the dingy lobby full of broken furniture and broken dreams. I saw young women, old women, and a handful of uneasy-looking men. The receptionist greeted me with a frown and gave me a clipboard of papers to fill out. I sat down with Jordan and we just looked at each. It seemed as if we were sitting in some type of death factory. I pictured in my mind that they removed pieces of your soul along with your unborn child. I got up quickly, returned the clipboard to the receptionist, and Jordan and I left hurriedly. I cried on the way home. Was I brave, or merely a spineless coward? All I knew is that Jordan was relieved, and I was still pregnant.

Reality returned as I lay in bed. I tried to comfort myself with food. I had gained ten pounds in four weeks, and for a model, that is not good. Once again I tried to find another abortion clinic. This time I called and spoke to someone over the phone. Her voice was sweet and melodic. I could hear her smiling through the phone, and I felt at ease talking to her. The next day, Jordan and I went to the office. We went up a dusty, winding staircase. The furniture was antiquated, but the office was orderly. The receptionist smiled sweetly and handed me a clipboard of paperwork. I filled out my medical history, and then we followed her to a room in the back with a desk, three chairs, and a TV. We waited there nervously until a nurse finally came in and said that to speak to a doctor, we would have to watch an "informational video" about abortion. The next thirty minutes were gruesome and appalling. The video looked as if it was from the 80s, and it showed dismembered fetuses in trash cans, terrifying instances of malpractice by doctors, and stories of women left for dead on operating tables. By the end of the video, I was sure I was going to puke. The nurse returned and asked quite soberly, "How do you feel?" I said, "I feel like the scum of the earth! I feel terrified. I feel awful!" The color had left Jordan's face. His eyes said enough. The nurse left again and said the doctor would be in shortly. As soon as the door closed, Jordan got down on both knees and buried his face in my lap, a torrent of tears streaming down his face as he cried, "Please, please, please, don't do this. I can take care of us. I want to marry you. I want to be a good father. Please, please, don't do this." I told Jordan to get up. I was angry with myself, with this clinic, with Jordan, and this nurse. When the doctor came in, I asked when I could schedule the procedure. She plainly told me that this was not an abortion clinic. She told me it was a Christian pregnancy center to prevent women from getting an abortion and that if I got an abortion, I would be, in her words, "doomed" to repeat the same mistake. I felt ambushed and deceived.

After a moment she asked if I would like a sonogram. I obliged, but I wasn't really sure why. "Why not?" I thought. Mentally battered, Jordan and I went to another room where I lay down and had cold gel squeezed over my bare belly. This was my "Twilight Zone," and I didn't know the way out. I wasn't prepared for what I saw and heard: a gentle, rhythmic thudding came from the machine. On the screen I could see a 3D image of what appeared to be a twinkling star in a faraway galaxy. This galaxy, of course, was my uterus, and this perplexing twinkling star was my baby. "My . . . *baby*?" I thought. I was awestruck. The heartbeat sounded like the most beautiful melody ever composed. Suddenly, my heart felt warm. The darkness began to melt. I couldn't explain my feelings. I felt like the Grinch: my heart was growing larger with each passing moment. Now I was sure I was in the proverbial twilight zone. They gave us a print out of the sonogram, wished us well, and we left.

In the car, Jordan snatched the sonogram out of my hands and ripped it up. "What's the point of keeping it if you're just going to get an abortion?" He was right, but why did I feel hurt? Why did I even care?

A week or so went by. My resolve was waning, so in a final attempt to "normalize" my life, I found another clinic and made another appointment. Ironically, it was right next door to the pregnancy center I had just visited. We waited about an hour before I could speak to a doctor. He then explained to me that I wasn't far along enough to require surgery, making me eligible for the abortion pill. He said it as if I had won some sort of prize in a sweepstake. He said it would be much safer than surgery and that it would be just like getting my period. "I'm sure," I thought sarcastically. A nurse then led me to a room where she explained what would happen next. She said I was required to take the first round of pills in front of her and then the following pills according to the scheduled dates. I checked the dates. The final date was Christmas. I shook my head fervently and said, "No, no, no. I can't have a miscarriage on Christmas." She then sternly told me that if I didn't take the pills today and the remaining pills accordingly, I would have to wait two weeks to reschedule an appointment, at which point I would be too far along to take the pills, so surgery would be necessary. I stared at her blankly. "Don't think too hard. Just do it." I thought. I took the pills and left.

Chris called me late Christmas Eve. He was on his way to Dallas. I tried to be as transparent as possible with Jordan and Chris. Jordan knew that I was still hopelessly in love with Chris. Chris knew that Jordan was hopelessly in love with me, and I just felt hopeless. In the early hours of Christmas morning, I invited Jordan over to be with me as I took the final pills. He brought movies, juice, and a pain reliever. What do you bring to soothe someone during a pre-meditated abortion? I was just happy he brought himself. I didn't want to be alone. The instructions required that the pills dissolve near your gum line so we waited . . . and waited. The cramping began lightly, but with each passing moment, the intensity grew. I was instructed by the nurse to take four Advils prior to consuming the pills. She assured me that this would be sufficient, but she was wrong. The pain became so unbearable that I began sobbing uncontrollably. The only way I could bear the pain was while I was on my knees. It was like I was already asking for forgiveness. Jordan began to cry; then we both cried. This went on for a while until Jordan gave me the pain relievers he had brought. By the time I awoke, it was daylight. Jordan was sitting in the corner of my room reading. He looked over to me as I stirred and smiled weakly. He held my hand and told me that he loved me. Jordan told my mother that I hadn't been feeling well and that he had come over to take care of me. When I woke up again, it was night and Jordan was gone.

Within a week, I moved out of my parents' house and into an apartment with Chris. The relief I initially felt after the abortion was dissipating. The dark cloud that hovered around me during my pregnancy began to grow. I knew something was terribly wrong, and I knew it was directly linked to the abortion. I spent a great deal of time crying in our closet. Where could I run? Whom could I tell my story to? I reached out to Jordan for any form of solace, but he had grown depressed as well. He had no more hope to offer me. My dream of having any sort of a "normal" life grew smaller with each passing day. Depression, shame, anger, and self-loathing began to consume me. Any mention of the "A" word to Chris was just a stark reminder of my betrayal of his love. As far as Chris was concerned, the past was the past, and it was time to move forward. I so desperately wanted to move forward, but I couldn't. I was stuck. I was anchored in grief and mourning because I knew—deep down inside—I had taken a precious, innocent life.

My relationship with Chris became very strained. We fought often. I had developed intimacy issues. So I drank. Drinking made me feel happy. It made me forget why I was crying in the closet. It helped me numb the pain of Christmas Day. Alcohol seemed like a viable solution, but underneath it all, darkness was still lurking. Eventually I became verbally abusive to Chris, calling him all the names I really wanted to call *myself*. The verbal abuse to Chris turned to physical abuse. I would experience fits of rage resulting in holes in the wall and shattered glass. Bruises, blisters, and scars were all over Chris' body. The cops visited regularly. I began to hate myself even more. How could I do this to someone I claimed to love?

The contempt and self-hatred I had for myself came to a boiling point. I began to self-mutilate. I carried a retractable razor in my purse. I hid loose razors around our house, just in case I needed one. I began to have panic attacks and chip my teeth from grinding them in my sleep. When I wasn't drinking or smoking marijuana, I would sleep ten to fifteen hours a day if I could. Eventually, I made an appointment with a psychiatrist. I explained my behavior to him, but I also said that I was a heavy drinker half-heartedly pursuing sobriety. By not being honest with the therapist, the medications he prescribed only compounded my issues.

Late one night, after an exceptionally volatile disagreement with Chris, I went to take a bath, but it was just an excuse for privacy so I could self-mutilate. This night, Chris opened the bathroom door, and what he saw frightened him so much that he called 911. When the police arrived, I was arrested and taken to a mental hospital in gel handcuffs. The experience at the hospital was sobering. By the time I returned home, I knew I needed real help, and that meant addressing my abortion.

Chris mentioned that he had seen a post-abortive recovery group in his church bulletin. He said it was worth looking into, and I agreed. I sent an email and received a prompt response. The day for the first class arrived, and I was elated. The women had been so courteous in trying to respect my privacy, but I didn't care if I had to shout it from the rooftops. I needed help. I wanted to live again. As I walked down the church hallway, I saw a smiling woman with brown hair. As silly as it may sound, it was like I was walking into a thousand sunrises. Her smile meant everything to me. I hadn't even walked into the classroom, and I already felt safe. The instructors were well-versed, compassionate, kind women from an organization called Peace After the Storm. They walked me and others through a nine-week Bible study that dealt specifically with the trauma abortion creates. During that nine-week journey toward healing, I was able to come to terms with the decision I had made to end my child's life. I was given many opportunities to express myself in a safe and healthy environment. Sure, there were many, many tears and much heartache as we uncovered the pain we all tried to bury for so long, but never once did I feel judged or afraid to speak the truth. The barrier that had grown in my spiritual life with God was being mended. I rededicated my life to Christ and was baptized again. I began to feel whole, healthy, and well. After the course was completed, I made the decision to enroll myself in an intensive outpatient program to address my issues with substance abuse.

The women of Peace After the Storm spoke life over me, and I will forever be grateful. They facilitated a healing process that brought restoration to my soul. Their passion for seeing the wounded and broken-hearted restored never ceases to amaze me. Their obedience to God to share their painful secrets has saved my life. I have witnessed the power of a person's testimony. The very thing you try to hide can be a lifeline for someone drowning in the sea of life. When I think of this ministry, I'm reminded of this verse, "And they overcame him by the blood of the Lamb, and by the word of their testimony . . ." (Rev. 12:11). Their bravery has taught me many things, but the one lesson that resonates with me the most is that fear is a liar. Decisions motivated by fear will always be regrettable.

A verse that often comes to mind is 1 Timothy 1:7: "For God has not given us a spirit of fear, but of power and of love and of a sound mind." So if fear isn't from God, why do we listen to it so often? I regret listening to the lies of fear, but I can feel at peace knowing that my child is in heaven, and one day, we'll meet again.

SHEA

Shea responded when one of our volunteers shared her story about our ministry in Sunday school. Shea's story confirms how the power of one person's experience can inspire you to further expand your own ministry.

* * *

As I sat in my Sunday school class one Sunday morning, a young lady got up to share the class's weekly Scripture verse as she did every week. After she cited the verse, she began to share about a ministry that had impacted her greatly. It was a ministry that offered Bible studies, encouragement, and support in helping women recover from the emotional trauma of having an abortion.

As I listened to the lady share her journey down the path of abortion and how the Lord had brought about a great restoration in her life, I wanted to stand up and say, "Way to go." I was so proud of her for sharing her story of God's restoration in her life. One never knows who is listening and may need healing in the same thing we have been through. As I listened to this young lady's testimony, it moved my heart even more, convincing me of the importance and need to share our stories of God's healing and redemption in our lives.

We make choices every day, and our choices—whether good or bad—will impact others. But one of the greatest choices we can make is to allow God to use us in telling others what He has done in and through our lives. We will impact a nation for Christ when we share His Gospel and redemption in our lives. I know this firsthand because I have lived it.

For many years I had a heart for reaching people for Christ. But not until a few years ago did I experience a true heart change. After many years of going back and forth in my walk with Christ, I rededicated my life to Him, and He began an amazing work. He stepped on the scene of my life and began to strip things from me that needed to go. Light has three functions, one of which is to reveal what is there. God turned on His light switch in my heart and revealed its true condition. He then began His work.

The molding and shaping process was difficult, yet so rewarding. For the next several years, God would work in my life in amazing ways. He would teach me the importance of forgiveness, the value of waiting rooms, the importance of prayer, and many other wonderful lessons. But there were a few gray areas I lived in, places I deemed small and insignificant. It would be months later that I would learn just how dangerous those gray areas really were.

Because true surrender under God's authority had never taken place, I would soon find myself wandering from my Father once again. I quickly found myself in a friendship with a married man. It started off very innocently, but would not end that way. I began to cross unhealthy boundaries such as texting and emailing this gentleman as well as confiding about personal problems. I had no business engaging in such things, yet I continued on, justifying every decision and every step taken. I did so because I thought I was too strong in the Lord to ever go back to a past God had delivered me from. I put no thought in needing to guard myself. I put my trust in myself in overcoming temptation instead of in God. My thought process had become incredibly tainted.

God was warning me to get out of this friendship, but I rationalized that it would be OK. In fact, I told God, "I've got this," and continued down the same path. Yet God's persistence—showing me red flags and convicting my heart—continued even as I ignored the Spirit's heeding.

It is of great importance to note that when God sees danger in our lives, He will caution us in many different ways. He reached out in every way possible to stop me from the hurt that was down the road, but I thought I knew best. Just like the prodigal son who decided to take a journey apart from his father's leading, I too took a journey that brought much hurt and pain to so many people.

I ended up stepping over an inappropriate line with this gentleman. And from that decision came one of the greatest times of brokenness in my entire life. I remember falling into my bed after stepping over the line and saying, "Lord, You won't forgive me this time." Yet to my amazement, He poured so much love into my heart and held me close through a very broken time in my life. I had broken His heart with my sin, but His love for me never changed.

I was in a ministry at the time, one which I loved with all my heart. I was serving under a board of directors who believed in me and in the ministry. I knew I had to go to each one and confess what I had done. And in time, I did.

Each board member began to pray for God's direction and leadership in handling the situation. This was a brand new ministry that was only a year old. I can't imagine the disappointment and hurt I caused each board member.

A meeting was called around Christmas—a time when most ministries come together to celebrate their year in ministry. However, this board had to decide what needed to happen to me regarding my role in the ministry as a result of my sin.

As each board member arrived at the home where the meeting was held, I found it difficult to keep my emotions in check. We all gathered in the host den. As I looked at each face, my emotions only grew stronger—emotions of regret and disappointment in letting down this board of directors who had believed in me. So, once again, I expressed how sorry I was and asked for their forgiveness. I then went downstairs as they talked about what needed to be done.

When the board called me back in to discuss their decision, the vice chairman, Mr. Brian, looked at me and said, "We are not going to fire you." After a moment, he added, "Shea, your life is more important than this ministry."

Not that the ministry wasn't important; that was not what he was saying at all. He was stressing that my life had meaning and value. To hear those words at a very broken time in my life showed me not only this man's character but also his reflection and love of Jesus Christ. Those words literally changed my life.

The board decided I needed to step down from speaking and leading Bible studies for a while, but they also decided they were going to stand by me. They never once stood for what I did, but they supported me throughout the restoration process. They walked alongside me through it all. I knew I deserved to be fired, but God had other plans.

As time went by, I suffered great consequences as a result of my sin. I lost the respect of others as well as a ministry I loved. The discipline of being broken and the resulting sadness was almost more than I thought I could bear. I remember thinking, "I may not make it through." But God's hands picked me up from out of a pit and showed me His love, mercy, and grace. From a time of repentance and brokenness came His forgiveness and restoration.

The restoration God brought to my life was what was most amazing. I never knew that God could do in a life what He did in mine, but He did, and it changed me forever. Rick Warren, author of The Purpose Driven Life, said, "Experience is not what happens to you. It is what you do with what happens to you. Don't waste your pain; use it to help others."[17]

---

[17] Rick Warren, *The Purpose Driven Life* (Grand Rapids, MI: Zondervan, 2002), 248.

The time came when God called me to share my story. He took me by the hand and led me through open doors to share His story for His glory. As I shared my testimony of restoration with others, I began to see God's hand at work in other people's lives. People were coming forward to share what the Lord had done in their lives as a result of hearing my testimony. God was working as only He could and changing hearts as only He can.

In 2 Corinthians 1:3-4, it states, "Blessed be the God and Father of our Lord Jesus Christ, the Father of mercies and God of all comfort, who comforts us in all our affliction so that we will be able to comfort those who are in any affliction with the comfort with which we ourselves are comforted by God."

I have moved forward with the Lord as He has continued to bring restoration to my life. If I am going to experience all that God has for me, then I must continue to move forward with Him. Paul said it best in Philippians 3:13: "Brethren, I do not regard myself as having laid hold of it yet; but one thing I do: forgetting what lies behind and reaching forward to what lies ahead."

So many people today are hurting in this world. They need to hear "there is hope." And when we share our stories of God's redemption and restoration, people will find hope. Sharing our stories is a powerful way to reach a nation for Jesus Christ. It can pave a way for the Gospel to be shared. I am so thankful for what He has done—and continues to do—in my life. I want to share with this world the love and restoration story of Jesus Christ.

My theme verse is Acts 20:24. It states, "But I do not consider my life of any account as dear to myself, so that I may finish my course and the ministry which I received from the Lord Jesus, to testify solemnly of the gospel of the grace of God." And this is what life is all about—sharing with others the Gospel message.

I believe there are many who feel God doesn't love them because of their past. They are living every day in defeat and in sadness. I want to share with them God's love for them and His desire to restore their lives. He is in the business of "lives being restored." I know this first-hand because I am a person He redeemed, rescued, and restored. I know my God today in a way I have never known before, and I will never be the same again.

As one of my favorite Rick Warren quotes says, "Other people are going to find healing in your wounds. Your greatest life messages and your most effective ministry will come out of your deepest hurts."[18]

[18] Ibid., 275.

PART III

TELL IT!

God whispers to us in our pleasures, speaks in our consciences, but shouts in our pains. It is his megaphone to rouse a deaf world.
–C. S. Lewis

CHAPTER 12
What Are We Talking About?

What I tell you in the darkness, speak in the light; and what
you hear whispered in your ear, proclaim upon the housetops.
–MATTHEW 10:27

You may be one of those readers who starts at the last chapter and works your way backwards. I hope not. I hope you are the type who starts at the beginning and stays on the "journey" without missing a chapter. By now, it is my hope you have begun to understand the power God has had in my life and the transformation He makes possible in the lives of those who respond to another person's sharing.

Our stories (yours and mine) were never intended to be kept under wraps. If you hold a candle and cover the flame with your other hand, preventing the flow of much-needed oxygen, the light will extinguish. The same goes for your testimony. If you don't share what God has done in your life, there are two losers: the recipient who doesn't hear your story, and you. The power of your story can be tremendous. It's really a continuation of the stories we read in the Bible, because the Bible is a tapestry of God's love for His creation, which includes you, me, and the next person.

Think about it: When God began to reveal Himself to the world, He did not send outlines and CliffsNotes. He began with a story. As a matter of fact, He created a huge picture of His love in the creation of the world and then placed a man and a woman inside that picture.

God wants us to share our stories of how He works in our lives. Scripture tells us: "and the life was manifested, and we have seen and testify and proclaim to you the eternal life, which was with the Father and was manifested to us. What we have seen and heard we proclaim to you also, so that you too may have fellowship with us; and indeed our fellowship is with the Father, and with His Son Jesus Christ" (1 John 1:2-3). In that text, John the apostle, who walked with Jesus, is now sharing his story with his readers. He was testifying, announcing the Good News to those who would listen. When we share the story of God's work in our own lives, we are sharing our own story. That's exactly what God expects from every believer—to simply share the Good News. He wants us to be witnesses to what we have seen Him do in our lives.

Most people attend church because someone shared their faith journey with them and invited them to visit, and that sharing and visit created a desire to change. No magic formulas, no special degrees, just a willingness to share the story of what God did in their own life—WE don't have to do anything except be willing to allow God to work through us and to share that experience to others. That's exactly how Christianity has been spread from the first day of the first church. Jesus would work in someone's life, and believers would simply share that story with others. Those early believers loved others enough to tell them the Good News and let God do the rest.

Let's face it, though, there are lots of people walking around who are afraid to share their stories for fear of judgment. Sadly, judgment can come from believers and non-believers alike.

It takes courage to divulge a secret you have held onto for years—something so personal, many would rather die than divulge their secret to anyone. But the power that comes for the one giving the testimony cannot be measured, and the healing is equally unmeasurable for those hearing the testimony.

In Luke 7:36-50, a woman who was notorious made a spectacle of herself in a passionate display of love and gratitude. Her regret was that she had offended God so grievously. Her joy was that Jesus forgave her sins and commended her for her great faith and love. It's a remarkable story:

> Now one of the Pharisees was requesting Him to dine with him, and He entered the Pharisee's house and reclined at the table. And there was a woman in the city who was a sinner; and when she learned that He was reclining at the table in the Pharisee's house, she brought an alabaster vial of perfume, and standing behind Him at His feet, weeping, she began to wet His feet with her tears, and kept wiping them with the hair of her head, and kissing His feet and anointing them with the perfume. Now when the Pharisee who had invited Him saw this, he said to himself, "If this man were a prophet He would know who and what sort of person this woman is who is touching Him, that she is a sinner."
>
> And Jesus answered him, "Simon, I have something to say to you." And he replied, "Say it, Teacher." "A moneylender had two debtors: one owed five hundred denarii, and the other fifty. When they were unable to repay, he graciously forgave them both. So which of them will love him more?" Simon answered and said, "I suppose the one whom he forgave more." And He said to him, "You have judged correctly." Turning toward the woman, He said to Simon, "Do you see this woman? I entered your house;

you gave Me no water for My feet, but she has wet My feet with her tears and wiped them with her hair. You gave Me no kiss; but she, since the time I came in, has not ceased to kiss My feet. You did not anoint My head with oil, but she anointed My feet with perfume. For this reason I say to you, her sins, which are many, have been forgiven, for she loved much; but he who is forgiven little, loves little." Then He said to her, "Your sins have been forgiven." Those who were reclining at the table with Him began to say to themselves, "Who is this man who even forgives sins?" And He said to the woman, "Your faith has saved you; go in peace."

You remember the story: This woman walked into a roomful of men where Jesus was reclining at a table. She held the most valuable possession she had, an alabaster jar of perfume. She knelt quietly at Jesus' feet as she covered his feet with kisses and then anointed his feet with the perfume. She had nothing else valuable to offer to show her overwhelming love and gratitude.

But Simon, good little Pharisee that he was, loved the law and all the regulations he lived by. They protected his sense of security; the law was his roadmap for righteousness, setting him apart from "ordinary" Jews. Why, Simon was appalled that a sinful woman would enter his house. This definitely offended his sense of order.

This woman recognized her desperate need for grace, and her repentance turned her world upside down, opening up an entirely new view of things. Our friend Simon, however, was religious and one who had done his best to live a respectable life. His sin was tucked away, hidden even from himself. His habit of judging others had formed a fence around his one-way view of the universe, insulating his neat and tidy life from the unpredictable power of grace.

But Simon and this woman were alike in that they both owed

a debt they could not possibly repay. Though Simon's sin was less obvious, it was also the more dangerous. He was a man following a map he thought would certainly lead to heaven—but when heaven came down and walked into his house, he didn't even recognize it. The woman, on the other hand, realized just how lost she had been. Forgiven much, she loved much. She found heaven at the feet of Jesus.

Let's be honest. Many of us (and I'm speaking to myself as well) would have responded to this sinful woman just as Simon did. It's so easy to look more with judgment than love at people whose lives have been devastated by sin. But Jesus looked at the hearts of this woman and at Simon and saw the same need: their need for forgiveness.

I believe that we are given this story so we can know that no matter how sinful, how broken, or how entrenched in error we might be, forgiveness is available if only we seek it in faith . . . that's a promise HE keeps on keeping.

CHAPTER 13
How to Tell It

And he who has seen has testified, and his
testimony is true; and he knows that he is telling
the truth, so that you also may believe.
–JOHN 19:35

The most effective method of sharing the Good News is sharing your personal story—simply sharing your spiritual pilgrimage. There will be skeptics and naysayers; people denying doctrinal truth, attacking the church, even attacking you, but no one—let me repeat, NO ONE—can deny what God has done in and through you. This is your testimony. This is YOUR story. You are the witness.

Many may turn "off," mentally and physically, when they see a preacher or evangelist get up to speak, but are somehow magically drawn to a human-interest story of how you—Mr. or Miss So-And-So—found peace or hope or renewed faith. Your story is compelling and plays at the strings of the heart, much the same way a symphony can sweep us off our feet.

The apostle Paul (you know the guy, Saul of Tarsus, who murdered Jews, and later met Jesus face to face on the road to Damascus) stood before six different audiences, alone, addressing masses of unbelievers and facing hostility, each time sharing his personal story.[19] That's right, each time Paul spoke, he simply shared how his own life had been changed by the power of Jesus Christ. Not once did he argue or debate with them. He didn't try to preach a sermon. Why? Because one of the most convincing, unanswerable arguments on earth regarding Christianity is one's personal experience with God. No persuasive technique will ever take the place of your testimony. I challenge you to give serious thought to analyzing and then presenting the way God saved you along with the exciting results of His presence in your life.

Paul was bold. He had an amazing transformation story to share, and he shared it short and to the point in each setting. By sharing your own journey, you "personalize" the Gospel message and its impact on people's lives today. In a sense, through hearing how God has worked in your life, people can visualize "God with skin on."

Someone told me recently a good verbal testimony should be Audible, Brief and centered on Christ. I thought this was pretty good–it's simple to remember, just A-B-C. You may want to throw in the following: be interesting (if you want someone to listen to you); be logical (if you want to be understood); be specific (to clearly explain your encounter); be practical (if you want your story to be used); be genuine (if you want results); and be respectful (never giving the impression you are judgmental).

Until the last few years, I was afraid to share my story. My life didn't match my talk. I got sidetracked and my life became messy. But when we are honest in our failures and point to the One who gives us victory over those failures, our story gains

[19] See Acts 22-26, the Holy Bible.

tremendous power.

Your story is the one that tells how His became Yours: how you were confronted by the grace of the Gospel and its life-giving message; how you finally understood the futility of your own attempts to look good to the world, yet not be in right standing before God; and how you finally ran with abandon into the open arms of the Savior. Sharing what God has done in your life is strategic in living out your faith. Your individual story makes up the greater story—the story of God's redeeming His people. Our stories encourage other believers while God also uses them to convert unbelievers to the faith.

Your faith story is an important tool in the hand of a mighty God: it can help others understand how God is also working in *their* lives.

CHAPTER 14
The Impact of Telling It

*I pray that the fellowship of your faith may
become effective through the knowledge of every
good thing which is in you for Christ's sake.*
−PHILEMON 1:6

No other person on earth knows you and your story better than you do. Sharing your story with others can be a powerful and important way to express your gratitude to God for all He has done.

Your story is not what a lawyer does. It's what a witness does. You're not trying to convince anybody. You're not trying to pressure someone for a decision. You're just telling others what happened to you. Nobody can tell your story because it's unique to you!

An attitude of gratitude is important as you share because you're expressing gratitude for what He has done in your life. An "attitude of gratitude" has been linked to better health, sounder sleep, less anxiety and depression, higher long-term satisfaction with life, and kinder behavior toward others. A study shows that gratitude makes people less likely to turn aggressive when provoked. "If you want to sleep more soundly, count blessings, not sheep."[20] Now this is a hidden health secret!

THE IMPACT OF OTHERS' STORIES

The impact of sharing your experience with others cannot be measured. Since early Christendom, one by one, people have shared their new found faith in Christ and sparked revival in others one story at a time . . . one person at a time. Here are a few examples of encouragement.

FROM ATHEIST TO AUTHOR

C. S. Lewis is one of the greatest defenders of the Christian faith in the twentieth century. His story is intriguing. Lewis left his childhood Christian faith to spend years as a determined atheist. After many years, Lewis finally admitted God existed and he gave in and knelt in prayer to become what he described later as "the most dejected and reluctant convert in all England."[21]

Lewis's long journey away from and back to faith began with his mother's death from cancer when he was a boy. Disillusioned that God had not healed his mother, Lewis set out on a path toward full-bodied rationalism and atheism. But the road back to faith was cluttered with obstacles Lewis thought were impossible to overcome. His conversion to a revived Christianity required years of intellectual battles that came only after being convinced that faith was reasonable.

Friendship is invaluable in communicating the Gospel, and

[20] John Tierney, "A Serving of Gratitude May Save the Day," *New York Times,* November 21, 2011, reporting on the book by Robert A. Emmons, *Thanks!: How the New Science of Gratitude Can Make You Happier* (Boston: Houghton Mifflin Harcourt, 2007).

[21] C. S. Lewis, *Surprised by Joy: The Shape of My Early Life* (New York: Harcourt, Brace, Jovanovich, 1966), 266.

Lewis found his friendships with Christians before coming to Christ deeply satisfying, as they shared interests on many levels. Christian friends such as J. R. R. Tolkien, Hugo Dyson, Owen Barfield, and others faithfully and patiently walked beside Lewis as they helped him resolve his many misgivings about Christianity. I'm certain these friends shared their own faith journeys with each other.

I'm inspired by the journey of C. S. Lewis, because through his many books, he provides valuable lessons for Christians today in sharing the Gospel with an unbelieving generation.

FROM SLAVE TRADER TO HYMN WRITER

I love music and especially hymns. One of the most beloved hymns of the Christian faith is "Amazing Grace." "Amazing grace, how sweet the sound, that saved a wretch like me . . ."[22] The author of the words was John Newton, a self-proclaimed wretch until his amazing conversion experience.

* * *

Newton was born in London July 24, 1725, the son of a commander of a merchant ship which sailed the Mediterranean. When John was eleven, he went to sea with his father and made six voyages with him before the elder Newton retired. In 1744, John was impressed into service on a man-of-war, the H. M. S. Harwich. Finding conditions on board intolerable, he deserted, but was soon recaptured and publicly flogged and demoted from midshipman to common seaman.

Finally, at his own request, he was exchanged into service on a slave ship, which took him to the coast of Sierra Leone.

---

[22] "English poet and clergyman John Newton (1725-1807) wrote the lyrics to this Christian hymn based upon his personal life experience.

He then became the servant of a slave trader and was brutally abused. Early in 1748 he was rescued by a sea captain who had known John's father. John Newton ultimately became captain of his own ship, one which plied the slave trade.

Although he had had some early religious instruction from his mother, who had died when he was a child, he had long since given up any religious convictions. However, on a homeward voyage, while he was attempting to steer the ship through a violent storm, he experienced what he was to refer to later as his "great deliverance." He recorded in his journal that when all seemed lost and the ship would surely sink, he exclaimed, "Lord, have mercy upon us." Later, in his cabin, he reflected on what he had said and began to believe that God had addressed him through the storm and that grace had begun to work for him.

For the rest of his life, he observed the anniversary of May 10, 1748, as the day of his conversion, a day of humiliation in which he subjected his will to a higher power. "Through many dangers, toils and snares, I have already come; tis grace has bro't me safe thus far, and grace will lead me home."[23] He continued in the slave trade for a time after his conversion; however, he saw to it that the slaves under his care were treated humanely.

He decided to become a minister and applied to the Archbishop of York for ordination. The Archbishop refused his request, but Newton persisted in his goal, and he was later ordained by the Bishop of Lincoln and accepted the curacy of Olney, Buckinghamshire. Newton's church became so crowded during services that it had to be enlarged. He preached not only in Olney but also in other parts of the country. In 1767 the poet William Cowper settled at Olney, and he and Newton became

[23] Ibid.

friends.

In 1780 Newton left Olney to become rector of St. Mary Woolchurch, in London. There he drew large congregations and influenced many, among them William Wilberforce, who would one day become a leader in the campaign for the abolition of slavery. Newton continued to preach until his last year of life, although he was blind by that time. He died in London on December 21, 1807. Slave trader, wretch turned minister in the Church of England, John Newton was secure in his faith with the assurance amazing grace would lead him home. Newton's simple faith in song has led countless home as well.

FROM TEENAGER TO GENERAL

William Booth was born in Nottingham, England in 1829. He was raised in the Church of England and "baptized" when he was two days old. His mother was a devout Christian. After his father's death, Booth was apprenticed to a pawnbroker and grew up in poverty. By the time Booth became a teenager, he was already interested in social reform and sought ways to alleviate the suffering of the poor. After breaking from the Church of England, he began attending Wesley Chapel of Nottingham. One night in 1844, when he was fifteen years old, Booth was saved at 11:00 p.m. on a street, coming home after services. Booth had a deep desire to win souls for Christ and walked the streets of London to preach the Good News to the poor, the homeless, the hungry, and the destitute. Timid at first, he finally ventured out to read the Bible and deliver messages on local street corners. Although jeered at and scorned, Booth was not discouraged. At seventeen, he preached his first sermon and was eventually licensed by the New Wesleyan Connexion.

Thieves, prostitutes, gamblers, and drunkards were some of Booth's first converts. Booth preached hope and salvation to the desperately poor. His desire was to lead people to Christ and link them to a church for further spiritual guidance. One day Booth brought a group of poor boys from the slums into the church. Unfortunately, this angered the minister, who asked them to come through the back door and sit where they couldn't be seen. Instead of becoming discouraged, Booth pressed on even harder, making hundreds of hospital calls to the sick and dying before he reached the age of twenty. Seeing London in 1849 was evidence to Booth of the great need so many had. "What a city to save!" said Booth.

In 1851, without a friend and almost broke, Booth was offered a pastorship in a Wesleyan Church group known as "Reformers." There he met his wife, Catherine. Eventually the Reformers joined the "Methodist New Connexion" movement in 1854. By now, Booth was gaining fame as a revivalist.

The great Salvation Army started July 2, 1865, as a large tent was erected on a Quaker burial ground in East London. Booth was now thirty-six years old. The "Army" was first called the East London (Christian) Revival Society, then the East London Christian Mission, then the Christian Mission. A chain of missions gradually formed, feeding and housing the poor and needy. But it did not come without opposition. It wasn't uncommon to see Salvationists with broken ankles and wrists. Eventually, "Salvation Army" was adopted as the title for the ministry. It was reorganized along the quasi-military lines of a well-disciplined army in 1878.

By 1879, "General" Booth had eighty-one stations, 127 full-time evangelists, and 75,000 services a year going. The "Army" expanded to the United States in 1880 and adopted uniforms. It is now an international organization.

"Go for souls, and go for the worst!" was the cry of Booth. The multitudes in London's slums convinced him he had discovered his calling, and no one ever took the Gospel to the "down and outer" like Booth did. Booth was once asked for the secret of his success:

> I will tell you the secret. God has had all there was of me. There have been men with greater brains than I, men with greater opportunities. But from the day I got the poor of London on my heart and caught a vision of all Jesus Christ could do with them, on that day I made up my mind that God would have all of William Booth there was. And if there is anything of power in the Salvation Army today, it is because God has had all the adoration of my heart, all the power of my will, and all the influence of my life.[24]

Well done, faithful servant! Booth had a powerful story to tell, he told it, and look at the results!

FROM HOPELESS TO A COMMUNICATOR OF HOPE[25]

Nick Vujicic is an amazing person. Nick was born in Melbourne, Australia, in 1982. Early sonogram technology failed to reveal that he had tetra-amelia syndrome, a rare disorder characterized by the absence of all four limbs. As you can imagine, Nick's story is compelling, revealing his struggle with depression and loneliness. He reached a low point where he wanted to commit suicide by drowning himself in the bathtub, believing his life had no purpose and he would never have someone to share life with. But he was wrong.

Today Nick is married, with an eighteen-month-old son. He

---

[24] "The Gospel Truth–William Bramwell Booth," *Gospeltruth.net,* http://www.gospeltruth.net/booth/boothbioshort.htm.

[25] "Man Without Arms and Legs Is Changing the World," Denison Forum on Truth and Culture, November 14, 2014, http://www.denisonforum.org/cultural-commentary/1240-man-without-arms-and-legs-is-changing-the-world.

is an author, international speaker, musician, and actor who enjoys fishing, painting, and swimming. In 2005 he established Life Without Limbs, an international non-profit ministry.

Nick says, "As a child I never thought I'd be any sort of communicator of hope, because I did not have any hope. I don't remember the last time I prayed for a miracle to have limbs, because I know I don't need limbs; I need peace. I don't need limbs; I need purpose. I don't need limbs; I need Jesus. And when you have Jesus, you have everything you need, because that is the only source of hope. If you have hope, you have everything, and Jesus is the hope."

Nick's story is a wonderful example of how one man's story can start a ministry, inspire so many, and impact millions around the world. He provides hope and reminds us there is no deformity in God's eyes.

But what if Nick had never shared his amazing story? The hope and encouragement he offers millions each time his story is shared is affecting our culture. His words enrich the lives of those who hear them.

If you think God cannot possibly use you for the kingdom, then think about Nick Vujicic's message: "If God can use a man without arms and legs to be His hands and feet, then he will certainly use any willing heart!"

FROM ATHEIST TO FAITH-BUILDER IN THE ENTERTAINMENT INDUSTRY[26]

Kirk Cameron is an actor working in an industry that is not known for its faith. In fact, the entertainment industry, by and large, is known for its *lack* of faith. Kirk grew up in a home

---

[26] "The Biggest Celebrity is Jesus," *Beliefnet*, http://www.beliefnet.com/Entertainment/Celebrities/The-Biggest-Celebrity-Is-Jesus.aspx#.

where no one attended church. He didn't believe in God and was an adamant atheist most of his life. He admits he was "too smart to believe in a fairy tale like that."

When Kirk was fourteen, he got a part on *Growing Pains*. It soon turned into a hit show. Kirk thought he had it made—as much money as he wanted, traveling worldwide—he was famous.

Then Kirk met the father of a girl he liked. That man, God bless him, said, "You have a lot, Kirk, but you don't have the Lord." Kirk didn't want any of this "God" thing, but he did want to date this man's daughter, so he accepted an invitation to attend church. While attending church for the first time, Kirk heard the Gospel. But instead of doing what you would think any hard-hearted, self-proclaimed atheist would do (not listen), Kirk DID listen and was caught off-guard. Kirk heard that the Bible was the Word of God. The preacher at that little church explained the Good News in a real and personal way, and Kirk Cameron was listening.

As Kirk listened, he realized that if what that preacher was saying was true, he was in big trouble. Kirk went home convicted of how he had been thinking and living. Naturally, Kirk had a lot of questions, so he asked his friend's father—about evolution, all kinds of religions, and the Bible. There was one question his friend's father asked Kirk that really made him think—whether or not God is real.

A pivotal moment came about a month later. Kirk was sitting in his car on the side of the road when he thought, If I get in a car accident and die today, will I be going to heaven? Kirk already knew the answer, and he knew it was time to do something about it. So he prayed, not knowing how, just talking to God from his heart. It wasn't an "ah-ha" moment for Kirk Cameron. No epiphany, no visions, but he KNEW God heard him and that He was listening. God was real.

Kirk shared his experience with a friend who was a Christian. Kirk was given a Bible and started reading it. He soon learned about an amazing God that loves us and cares for us. Today, Kirk Cameron shares his story of faith freely to all. He says, "Nothing compares to the joy of knowing Jesus Christ, of knowing that my sins are forgiven and that I'm in a right relationship with God."

FROM LEFTIST PROFESSOR TO DEVOTED FOLLOWER[27]

As a professor of English and women's studies, on the track to becoming a tenured professor, Rosaria Champagne Butterfield cared about morality, justice, and compassion. Fervent for the world views of Freud, Hegel, Marx, and Darwin, she stood with the disempowered and valued morality. She got turned off by Christians because she felt they were too dogmatic and "Republican." A self-proclaimed leftist, lesbian professor, she felt her life was happy, meaningful, and full. She stood up for good causes and felt she was a good citizen and caregiver.

In her research surrounding the Religious Right and what she perceived to be their own politics of hatred, she knew she would need to read the Bible, which she considered had gotten many people off track. Her first article attacked the Promise Keepers and was published in 1997. Her article generated a lot of mail—both for and against her position. But she received one letter from a pastor of a Presbyterian church she could not file away. His letter was kind and inquiring, not like the others she had received. His letter didn't argue, but it simply asked her to defend the foundation upon which the article was

---

[27]Rosaria Champagne Butterfield, "My Train Wreck Conversion," *Christianity Today* 57, no. 1 (January/February 2013), 112.

based. Not knowing how to respond, Rosaria threw the letter away.

But later in the evening, Rosaria pulled the letter out of the trash and set it aside. After all, Rosaria was an intellectual, a professor, and she operated under a different worldly view, not under a supernatural one shared by Christians. The pastor's letter put a hole right through the heart of her project.

Over the course of a few years, the pastor from the little church brought the church to Rosaria. He didn't mock her; instead, he invited her to get together for dinner. Rosaria's intentions were purely for research. But something else happened. The pastor and his wife became friends with Rosaria, entering her world. They met her friends. They talked openly about sexuality and politics. When they broke bread, the pastor would pray intimately. The pastor was revealing his God to Rosaria as holy and firm, yet full of mercy. Rosaria felt it was safe to be friends with him.

Soon Rosaria started reading the Bible. She was a voracious reader, reading the Bible through many times in multiple translations. At a gathering with her partner and a transgendered friend, a comment was made that the Bible was changing her. Rosaria had wondered the same thing. If Jesus was real, were they all in trouble?

Continuing her reading, she was battling the idea that the Bible was inspired. The words were overflowing into her world. One Sunday she left her partner and soon found herself sitting in the pew of that little Presbyterian church. One Sunday, the preacher spoke on John 7:17: "If anyone wills to do [God's] will, he shall know concerning the doctrine." Rosaria wanted God to show her why homosexuality was a sin. She wanted to judge, not be judged. Pondering question upon question, she prayed for willingness to obey before she understood. Who was she? Whom would God have her to be?

Then, on an ordinary day, Rosaria came to Jesus, without fear. The preacher and his wife were there. The church faithful, who had been praying for her for many years, were there. Jesus triumphed in that Rosaria was a broken mess waiting to be put together by a loving God. Rosaria believed that if Jesus could conquer death, he could make right her world. Rosaria drank the Living Water and rested in the shelter of her covenant family, where she resides still.

FROM ATHEIST LEGAL AFFAIRS JOURNALIST TO PREACHER AND AUTHOR

Lee Strobel, Christian author and apologist, was a lifelong skeptic and self-proclaimed atheist most of his life. As Strobel writes in the introduction of *The Case for Christ*, "As far as I was concerned, the case was closed. There was enough proof for me to rest with the conclusion that the divinity of Jesus was nothing more than the fanciful invention of superstitious people . . . or so I thought."[28] In writing *The Case for Christ*, Strobel used his skills as a legal affairs journalist to weigh in on the evidence for the existence of Christ as he presented his case before you and me, the jurors, to convince us that Christ was a myth. In trying to prove his case, he found new faith and met Christ up close and personal in a very real way. Lee Strobel, co-founder of the Institute at Cherry Hills in Colorado, is now one of the leading defenders of Christianity through his books and lectures. "Nobody is beyond the reach of the Gospel," says Strobel.[29]

---

[28]Lee Strobel, *The Case for Christ* (Grand Rapids, MI: Zondervan, 1998), 15.

[29]Alex Murashko, "Lee Strobel Weighs in on How Atheist Activist Can Turn Christian," *The Christian Post*, April 6, 2012.

FROM PRODIGAL TO PREACHER[30]

If I say the name Tullian Tchividjian you may say, "Who is that?" But if I say the name Billy Graham's grandson, you'd probably say, "Oh, wow!" Tullian was raised in a warm, caring Christian family but rejected everything he was raised to know and believe. Young, sixteen-year-old Tullian was rebellious to the point of tearing his family apart. He never doubted the existence of God. He believed in the Bible and Jesus and the cross. He simply wanted to have fun and live freely to do whatever he wanted. Tullian's greatest fear was that a surrendered life would mean loss of the fun and excitement this world has to offer.

Tullian would stay with families of friends, but soon, they would kick him out, too. He dropped out of high school and worked at restaurants and in construction. But instead of paying his bills and rent, he wasted his money on drugs, alcohol, and girls. He was an admitted thief.

One day he met Kim, who waitressed at a local restaurant. She was attracted to Tullian but knew he needed some growing up. Eventually, Tullian and his parents reconciled, and before long, Kim had dinner at their home. Kim was a positive influence on Tullian. By the time he reached twenty-one, he was more responsible, paying his bills, holding down jobs, and maturing. Tullian instinctively knew there must be more to life than what this world was offering.

One night, Tullian came to a breaking point, and on bended knee, yielded himself to God to make changes in his life. It was then that his thinking and attitudes changed. He no longer had the desires of this world. He loved the things he used to hate

---

[30]Shannon Woodland with Tim Branson, "Tullian Tchividjian: Prodigal Grandson Comes Home," *CBN.com*, http://www.cbn.com/700club/features/amazing/tullian_031308.aspx.

and hated the things he used to love. Kim also gave her life to Jesus Christ.

Tullian and Kim were married by Tullian's grandfather, Billy Graham; Tullian later attended college, seminary, and graduate school. He now pastors New City Church in Coconut Creek, Florida, where he shares his grandfather's mission to see all come to Jesus Christ.

Tullian's life is proof that when God gets hold of a willing heart, your life will change.

FROM WHITE HOUSE SPECIAL COUNSEL TO INTERNATIONAL PRISON MINISTRY

Chuck Colson was White House Special Counsel to President Richard Nixon during the Watergate scandal. He was known as a "hatchet man" and "ruthless." In 1974, he was at the top of the world, yet feeling that something was missing. When Chuck left the White House and resumed his private legal practice, he was meeting with Tom Phillips, then president of Raytheon Corporation. Chuck remembered Tom was more at peace than ever before. When Chuck asked why, Tom said he had given his life to Christ. When Chuck's world turned topsy-turvy following the Watergate investigations and it looked like he would be facing prison, Chuck met with Phillips again. Phillips took a few moments to read from a chapter titled "The Great Sin" in C. S. Lewis' book *Mere Christianity*:

> There is one vice of which no man in the world is free; which every- one in the world loathes when he sees it in someone else; and of which hardly any people, except Christians, ever imagine that they are guilty themselves . .. There is no fault which makes a man more unpopular, and no fault which we are more unconscious of in ourselves ... The vice I am talking of is Pride or Self-Conceit:

and the virtue opposite to it, in Christian morals, is called Humility.[31]

Hearing these words, Colson said he knew "it was me Lewis was writing about." As Chuck drove away from Phillips' home that night, he stopped the car and cried out to God to forgive his sins.

For the remainder of Colson's life, he expressed gratitude for the Watergate debacle, because that experience set his life on a new course. He was sentenced to three years in federal prison for obstruction of justice, serving seven months of that sentence. But throughout that time, God gave Chuck Colson a new mission of ministering to prisoners. Within months, Prison Fellowship was born. That ministry has now grown into a large and well-respected outreach to prisoners around the world. "One of the greatest things that happened in my life was going to prison," he said.

In Chuck's own words: "I've just been a man doing his duty. When I think of what my Savior did for me . . . I would be dead today were it not for that. I would have suffocated in the stench of my own sin. I do what I do out of gratitude to God for what He's done for me."[32]

Well done, faithful servant!

FROM ATHEIST TO PRO-LIFE ADVOCATE

You may have never heard of Norma McCorvey, but you probably *have* heard of her legal pseudonym, Jane Roe. Norma was the plaintiff in the landmark Supreme Court decision *Roe v. Wade* in 1973, which overturned individual states' laws against

[31] C. S. Lewis, *Mere Christianity,* (New York: Harper Collins, 1952), 103.

[32] Chuck Colson, *Chuck Colson Speaks* (Urichsville, OH: Barbour Publishing, 2000), 137.

abortion by ruling them unconstitutional. Norma never had an abortion, but gave birth to a girl who was put up for adoption. In the 1980s, Norma revealed herself to be the "Jane Roe" of the famous lawsuit, telling the story behind the lawsuit of how she was the subject of two young and ambitious lawyers who were looking for a plaintiff with whom they could challenge the Texas state law prohibiting abortion.

By 1994, Norma renounced her atheism and converted to Christianity. She continues to express remorse over her part in the Supreme Court decision and now is a leading spokesperson against abortion through her Dallas ministry, Roe No More Ministries.

FROM BARTENDER TO FAITH-FILLED TV DYNASTY

Phil Robertson, the "Duck Commander," is the founder of a business empire and patriarch of a large Southern family. When he was in his late twenties, he was living a "sex, drugs, and rock and roll," lifestyle and running a local bar. One day a guy walked in carrying a Bible and wanted to talk to Phil. Phil ran him off, but one day looked him up again when Phil's life turned from bad to worse.

Phil was twenty-eight he first heard about "this guy called Jesus." On that day, Phil Robertson turned his life over to this Jesus, God in flesh, and let Him change his lifestyle. Phil took a leap putting his faith in this Jesus, but he was grateful that Jesus, God in flesh, paid the price for a "scumbag like me."

Phil is older and has a large family now. Week after week, millions watch this family tell their story as they end each segment of "Duck Dynasty" in prayer around their dining room table.

FROM HOPELESS TO INTERNATIONAL APOLOGIST[33]

Ravi Zacharias was born in Madras, India, one of four siblings. Zacharias claims descent from a woman of the Nambudiri Brahmin caste and Boatman caste. Swiss German missionaries spoke to one of his ancestors about Christianity, and his family was converted.

Zacharias grew up in a nominal Anglican household and was a practicing atheist until the age of seventeen. Often disappointing his father, Ravi was frequently beaten. His sisters convinced him to go to a Youth for Christ rally. Ravi was the only one to walk forward to receive Christ that night. Later that year, Ravi attempted suicide. A Youth for Christ worker visited him in the hospital, reading John 14 to him. Ravi says that it was John 14:19 that touched him. That single Scripture means so much to him he considers that his defining moment: "Because I live, you also will live." Ravi left the hospital a transformed seventeen-year-old. He thought, "This may be my only hope: A new way of living. Life as defined by the Author of Life." He committed his life to Christ, praying, "Jesus, if You are the one who gives life as it is meant to be, I want it. Please get me out of this

hospital bed well, and I promise I will leave no stone unturned in my pursuit of truth." In 1966 Zacharias immigrated with his family to Canada, where he earned his undergraduate degree from Ontario Bible College in 1972 (now Tyndale University College & Seminary) and his master of divinity degree from Trinity International University.

---

[33] Ravi Zacharias, "Antidote to Poison," *Christianity Today*, April 26, 2013, http://www.christianitytoday.com/ct/2013/april/antidote-to-poison.html; "In Search of Eden," The Gideons International Blog, April 4, 2014, http://blog.gideons.org/2014/04/in-search-of-eden-ravi-zacharias-testimony/.

Ravi has published twenty-eight books and is an international speaker and Christian apologist. Is he making a difference in sharing his story and his faith? You bet!

FROM ALCOHOLIC TO A WORLD CHANGING MOVEMENT[34]

Norm Miller started working at Interstate Batteries as a battery salesman. He progressed to selling and setting up Interstate distributorships. Before long, he started drinking, needing alcohol to function.

Norm had been drinking heavily one night when he was stopped by police. Fortunately for him, the officer didn't check his record for previous convictions, so he didn't find two DWIs on his record. That was the turning point. Realizing how low he had fallen with his drinking, he cried out, "God help me! I can't handle it!" Within days, a friend told Norm to read the Bible.

Norm paid attention to what his friend said, and the more he read, the more he realized the Bible was true.

One Sunday, Norm heard a Sunday school lesson about God's love for us. "How could God love me?" says Norm. "I lived totally for myself. I was selfish and broken." Soon after, Norm was at a friend's Bible study, and the man helped Norm make the most important decision in his life.

Norm always measured how successful he was by how much he earned. But once Norm made a decision for Christ, changes began. Instead of measuring his worth by dollar signs, Norm started to measure how much he was experiencing God's love and how he was showing that love to others.

Eventually, Norm became chairman of Interstate Batteries. By this time, Norm's faith had grown to the point he was not shy

---

[34] Norm Miller, *Beyond the Norm* (Nashville: Thomas Nelson Publishing, 2009), 42.

about sharing his faith. In his own words, Norm says, "I want to be known not just as the guy who sold batteries but also as a man who shared God's love."

When Norm turned seventy, he realized his clock was ticking (I can relate to this). He remembered the Scripture that said we are all to be witnesses all over the earth. So Norm wanted to share Jesus to the people in the Dallas area. Norm thought about how he would lift Christ up to others. "What would I do to sell more batteries? I would do a media campaign. Maybe that's what I need to do for Christ."

So Norm founded I Am Second (God Is First, I Am Second) in 2008. What started as a media campaign in Dallas at twenty churches is now in over 212 countries with over seven million hits on their website. Most visitors stay over seven minutes. I would say Norm has learned the importance of sharing a story.

THE ROAD TO WORLDWIDE EVANGELIST

There is one more story to share. Billy Graham's estimated lifetime audience, including radio and television broadcasts, topped 2.2 billion as of 2008. That's a big number and hard to fathom. But the story behind Billy's road to becoming the world's best known evangelist is nothing short of amazing.

* * *

Edward Kimball was a Sunday school teacher who not only prayed for his group of rowdy boys in his Sunday school class but also sought to win each one over to the Lord. One of his boys, in particular, didn't seem to understand what the Gospel was about, so Kimball went to the shoe store where one of his "rowdies" was stocking shelves and confronted him in the stock room with the importance of a personal relationship with Jesus Christ. That young man was Dwight L. Moody. Moody would become an evangelist reaching two continents for God. That's where the story begins.

There was another man working under Moody named Wilbur Chapman. Chapman later became an evangelist preaching to thousands. One day at one of his revivals, a professional ball player had a day off and attended one of Chapman's revival meetings. That ball player was Billy Sunday.

Sunday quit baseball and became part of Chapman's evangelistic team. Over time, Billy Sunday held his own crusades. One of the converts at a Billy Sunday revival was Mordecai Ham.

When Mordecai Ham came to Charlotte, North Carolina, a sandy-haired, lanky young man in high school vowed that he would never set foot to hear Mordecai preach. But his friends were going, so Billy Frank, as he was called by his family, went too.

Billy was intrigued by what he heard, so he went another night, responded to the invitation, and was converted. Billy Frank, known as Billy Graham, would preach to more people than any other person who ever lived over the next fifty years.

It all started with one Sunday school teacher's love for his boys. And so it is with the influence of a single person.

The stories above give you a glimpse of changed lives and the power they have on others. What do they have in common? Rich, poor, old, young, with limbs or without—God has used ordinary people in extraordinary ways to reach others. In every instance they each become honest about their need for a loving God; listened to Him more than they talked; and offered God their complete, unhesitating obedience. What happened to each of them can happen to you.

CHAPTER 15
Your Turn to Tell It

For whatever is born of God overcomes the world; and this is the victory that has overcome the world—our faith.

–1 JOHN 5:4

You've made it—the last chapter! But my job in writing *Go Tell It!* wouldn't be complete unless I shared the most important part of the story—the victory.

There have been many times I have reached a fork in the road with a major decision in front of me and I ask, "Which path do I take?" Do I take the path that is well travelled, that I know will get me to my destination eventually? Or, do I take the path that could be quicker, though unfamiliar, and have the potential for trouble? You may have experienced similar experiences.

This describes life pretty well. It certainly does mine. If we are honest, we are all confronted with decisions in life and the question of which path to take. I have been on a path for a few years now, starting a post-abortion ministry in unfamiliar (and often unwanted) territory. And by my very nature, I always have questions.

But God is good and provides the answers before the questions can even be asked. A few weeks ago, an older woman (in her seventies) approached me at church. She said, "I need to tell you something. When I was young, I had an abortion and I lived with that pain for over fifty years until I went through a recovery Bible study like yours. Bless you, honey. Keep doing what you're doing." I thanked her, hugged her, turned and gave a big thank you to the "Man Upstairs."

More answers came at the conclusion of two recovery groups. There had been amazing transformation in the recovery participants. Each unique . . . each with their own story . . . each finding their voice to be able to share the transformation they experienced with others.

I went to a church bazaar a few months ago. I was in a hurry and didn't expect to find anything (other than food) to purchase, when I literally stumbled on the last table by the door. A lovely young woman was there with unique artwork I hadn't seen elsewhere. In speaking with her, she shared how she came to accept Christ as her Savior . . . through a post-abortion Bible study.

How do I know I'm on the right path? How do I know I'm following God's will for my life and not my own? This is my non-theology answer: as long as I do something to build up the kingdom, and it is not contrary to His Word, and He continues to open and close doors, all I have to do is keep walking.

God revealed himself to me over the years, chipping away at walls I had built, until such time I turned over a secret so well hidden I thought I would take it to my grave. But secrets and isolation kill. And God didn't want that. Betsie ten Boom, the Dutch Christian Corrie ten Boom's sister, once said, "[T]here is no pit so deep that He [God's love] is not deeper still."[35] I had dug

<hr />

[35] "Corrie ten Boom," *tlogical.net*, http://www.tlogical.net/bioboom.htm. Corrie ten Boom (1892-1983) and her sister Betsie were held in several prisons and concentration camps for providing sanctuary to Jewish residents of Holland during World War II. These were some of the last words Betsie spoke to Corrie before dying at Ravensbruck, a women's concentration camp in northern Germany, on December 16, 1944.

a deep pit for myself, but Jesus was more than able to pull me out and fill my void with love.

Today I am a changed person. Once an angry, empty, fearful, hopeless, rebellious young girl, I'm now a secure, hopeful, peaceful, and joy-filled woman of God (notice I didn't say perfect. I am and always will be imperfect). Impossible for us to accomplish, but always possible for Jesus.

Will there be storms in our lives? Most certainly. Today, though, I weather the storms not because of "who *I* am," but because of "*whose* I am." Looking back over my life, I now see His hand weaving a beautiful tapestry in my life. God was at work in the details by helping me reconcile with my parents, blessing me with a wonderful son, bringing Cary and his children into my life, teaching me how to have a relationship, helping me to make amends to people I had hurt, and seeking honesty with myself and others. God was at work in the details as Cary led my ex-husband to faith in Christ, even delivering the eulogy at his funeral, while providing an earthly father for my son. God was at work in me this year as I weathered the storm of cancer. And God is continually at work in me as I continue to share what He's done in my life. Those truths can be the same for you.

Now to the best part. There's another book I want to talk about. It's not a book of fairy tales but one filled with stories of ordinary people who were used in extraordinary ways by a very awesome God. One story in particular is the miracle of a baby's birth in a stable in Bethlehem. That baby is Jesus, and that baby, as much God as he was man, grew to walk this earth to willingly sacrifice Himself on a cross for you and me. The miracles of change that happened in my life can happen in yours, too. Whatever your circumstance, whatever you've done or didn't do, doesn't matter. What does matter is having the desire to know God through faith in Jesus Christ: not in your head, but in your heart.

This Jesus I'm talking about is ready to meet you. No high-pressure sales, just a gentle knock on the door of your heart. All you have to do is ask. All you need is a humble spirit and an honest desire to put Him first. There's no special words or fancy formula required, just talking from your heart to God's ears.

This much I know . . . there will be storms in life. I absolutely know this! I do not know what tomorrow will bring, but I do know Who holds tomorrow. Share your faith . . . share your story . . . *Go Tell It!*

> *He is no fool who gives what he cannot keep*
> *to gain that which he cannot lose.*
> –JIM ELLIOT[36]

---

[36] Jim Elliot (1927-1956) was a missionary to the Huaorani people of Ecuador in 1956. During a mission trip known as "Operation Auca," Elliot and four other men were murdered by Huaorani warriors shortly after making initial contact. His widow, Elisabeth Elliot, published several books that included his letters and journals.

GO TELL IT ON THE MOUNTAIN[37]

Go, tell it on the mountain,
Over the hills and everywhere
Go, tell it on the mountain,
That Jesus Christ is born.

While shepherds kept their watching
Over silent flocks by night
Behold throughout the heavens
There shone a holy light.

Go, tell it on the mountain,
Over the hills and everywhere
Go, tell it on the mountain,
That Jesus Christ is born.

The shepherds feared and trembled,
When lo! above the earth,
Rang out the angels chorus
That hailed the Savior's birth.

Go, tell it on the mountain,
Over the hills and everywhere
Go, tell it on the mountain,
That Jesus Christ is born.

Down in a lowly manger
The humble Christ was born
And God sent us salvation
That blessed Christmas morn.

Go, tell it on the mountain,
Over the hills and everywhere
Go, tell it on the mountain,
That Jesus Christ is born.

---

[37] African-American spiritual song, compiled by John Wesley Work, Jr., dating back to at least 1865.

Dear reader,

Thank you for sharing this time together. It is my hope that you learned something along the way.

My life story navigates around a central theme, that of making peace with your past. Such a large portion of my life was robbed of joyous living because I chose to protect my "secret" instead of being completely transparent with God and others.

This much I know: At the end of my life, when I am a breath away from meeting my Maker, I do not want regrets remaining. I want to run to Jesus and have Him say, "Well done, good and faithful servant."

My prayer is that you will say the same.

Until next time . . .

Debby